"I grew up listening to many things.
My father always told us that the world
does not stop at our doorstep."

Angélique Kidjo, p. 96

Contents

ON THE COVER

When you really dig into the roots of music around the world, so much of it comes down to the way people interacted centuries ago, when someone set out across the sea (or land) and wound up elsewhere. The story of music, after all, is the story of humanity and its journey around the globe; the story of what's "here" and the wondering about what's "over yonder." For the cover of our issue about roots music beyond the US, we turned to Cork, Ireland-based illustrator Craig Carry for an image that could pull together the ideas of exploring outside the US and music's journey around the world. He gave us a winding road, a sailing ship, wind wafting off the shore, birds migrating, and a red sunset over mountains.

Inside covers:
Lyrics from Angelique Kidjo's "Ife."
Illustrations by Drew Christie.

Dear reader,

While we were making this issue, we learned of the passing of my dear friend and brother-in-bluegrass Denis Gainty. You may have read Denis' introduction to the history of bluegrass in Japan in our Spring 2016 issue, and you can read his profile of Japanese legends Bluegrass 45 on page 124 of this issue. Denis was working on a book about bluegrass music in Japan. He's survived by his two children and countless students and friends in the US, Japan, and elsewhere. We're grateful to have been able to provide some space for his writing. May he rest in peace.

Sincerely,

Chris Wadsworth
Publisher of *No Depression*

NO DEPRESSION TEAM
Chris Wadsworth *Publisher*
Kim Ruehl *Editor-in-Chief*
Stacy Chandler *Assistant Editor*
Cameron Matthews *Editor of NoDepression.com*
Sonja Nelson *Advertising*
Henry Carrigan *Print Partnerships*
Maureen Cross *Finance/Operations*

WEB nodepression.com
TWITTER & INSTAGRAM @nodepression
FACEBOOK facebook.com/nodepressionmag

GENERAL INQUIRIES
info@nodepression.com

ONLINE ADVERTISING
advertising@nodepression.com

SUBSCRIPTIONS
nodepression.com/subscribe

JOURNAL DESIGN & PRODUCTION
Marcus Amaker
Printed in Canada by Hemlock Printers , 100% carbon neutral

No Depression is part of the FreshGrass Foundation.
freshgrass.org
ISBN-10:0-9973317-9-8
ISBN-13:978-0-9973317-9-0
©2017, FreshGrass, LLC

Hello Stranger

BY KIM RUEHL

The world, right? Where does one even start?

For a long time, we in the roots music community have tooled along under the assumption that, in the realm of traditional music, there is American roots music, which is, more or less, a very specific, concentrated category, and then there's world music, which is everything else in the world. When you really think about it, though, the way we've sliced these categories seems a bit silly.

After all, the story of a band like Hanggai, whom you can read about on page 132, is not unlike the story of, say, Rhiannon Giddens, American folksinger. Both grew up as minorities, learning about the culture and music of their ethnic majority neighbors. Both became musicians within that paradigm before immersing themselves in the traditional music of their minority culture. Both dedicated their lives and careers to bringing forward those traditions, rich and deep in their meaning and influence. That one sings in English and the other in Mongolian is a minor detail when you consider the broad, universal commonality present in the music. So why does one get marketed in a specific, digestible category while the other is sold stateside as something foreign, exotic, unknown?

That's the question we wanted to explore in this issue, which I've been telling friends is about "roots music around the world." When they invariably respond with one of two statements — "Like Australian Americana?" or "I love world music!" — I've had to back up a little and explain.

To most musicians, there is no "us and them," only, "Can you show me how to play that thing?" It's the media, the industry, the marketers, the fans who feel the need to categorize, for the sake of discussion. But does that really serve the experience of hearing music, or making it? If I tell you this CD I'm going to play is from far away, in a different language, doesn't that set you up to view it as foreign and exotic, rather than just another person in another place sharing how they feel through melody and rhythm?

It's easy, when we don't have firsthand experience with something, or when we're afraid of the unknown, to place people and even entire cultures into categories. Lumping an entire world of traditional music into one category is a bit like calling all people with brown skin "foreigners." What do we even mean by that? What is the purpose? Is that productive in any way? These are all questions that music can

guide us through. And lately, it's become clear, these are questions that come up not only in the context of exploring roots music around the world, but also just in waking up in the morning, checking the news.

Once again, we didn't plan an issue to be so timely. We were just curious about the Hanggais of the world, the Puente Celestes and Parekh & Singhs, the Yirrmals. We were curious about how they were tapping into the long, storied traditions of their people and pulling them into the future. As I told Richard Shindell during our interview, we were looking for the Chris Thiles of other countries. Inadvertently, we wound up unearthing stories that run parallel to the most pressing issues of the day.

Many times in the making of this issue, I've thought about what Mark Twain once said: "Travel is fatal to prejudice, bigotry, and narrow-mindedness, and many of our people need it sorely on these accounts. Broad, wholesome, charitable views of men and things cannot be acquired by vegetating in one little corner of the earth all one's lifetime."

Of course, travel can be expensive and arduous and challenging. Luckily, even when we don't have the time or money to afford it, music can take us there. Turn the page and turn up the tunes. It's all just people, singing songs.

NO DEPRESSION

Janka Nabay

SOUND CARRIES

Immigrants carve new niches for music from their homelands

by Megan Romer

NEW YORK CITY'S MOST dedicated music enthusiasts know that if you want to hear the really *really* good stuff, you skip "world music night" and similar events at Lincoln Center or Carnegie Hall and instead hop on the train to the outer boroughs. For an evening of Ghanaian music, find a dancehall in the Bronx's Melrose. Want to dig through massive crates of hard-to-find Haitian and Trinidadian CDs? Head to Flatbush, Brooklyn. The real beneficiaries of the music that fills these enclaves are not visiting crate-diggers, though; they're the actual members of these communities, for whom music is a connection to home and to each other.

Despite waves of anti-immigrant sentiment throughout American history, immigration persists, and musicians who perform the music of their home countries in the United States are planting new roots as they do so — through bhangra and reggaeton, pinoy rock and pansori. They fold these styles into the idiom that is contemporary American music, some of which will grow organically, some of which will be snatched up and commodified by pop producers seeking flavor for their next radio hit.

Regardless of what the music industry does, immigrants find some of their most powerful and poignant moments of community when their musicians take the stage. As a result, artists like Honduran-born, part-time Brooklynite Aurelio Martinez (known simply as Aurelio) find themselves playing in more than one context.

"I do music two ways," says Aurelio. "Sometimes I play in Manhattan, [in] Carnegie Hall," where, he explains, his fellow Garifuna expats largely cannot afford to purchase tickets and the rows of seats don't make for good dancing space anyway. Thus, in the concert hall, he tailors his performance to the mostly white ticket-buying crowd who want to hear folkloric elements at the forefront, tricky instrumental work, and as much inter-song explanation as possible.

But Aurelio also plays occasional club shows in New York City's outer boroughs, which aren't advertised to the NPR-listening set, but rather cater to the expatriate Garifuna community — an Afro-Caribbean culture that was displaced to Central America after descending from the survivors of a wrecked slave ship and the native Carib and Arawak people who took them in.

At the Garifuna shows, and at all of his shows back home in Honduras, Aurelio says he plays "punta rock," a modernized version of the folkloric stuff, made for dancing. He loves both the traditional and modernized styles (and the differences between the two are ultimately fairly subtle, especially to the outsider's ear), and says, "It's wonderful to bring the music out — to see [non-Garifuna] people enjoy it — but it's also so nice to play our music in our way." In both contexts, he finds that his messages of inclusivity and social justice resonate, and his recorded work (including a release last spring titled *Darandi*) features these themes heavily.

"When I write songs, I talk about social problems. ... God created one world for everybody, but we have to be free. My history, the history of the Garifuna people, it comes from immigrants, and also from people who never wanted to leave a place but had to learn to live in a new place," he says, referencing the multiple displacements he and so many of his ancestors have experienced in one way or another. This specific sentiment may not be universal, but the pull of freedom is certainly one that all people can understand.

"Humans must learn to be like the birds," he says. "No walls, no fences. Just fly above." Aurelio echoes this in one of his best-known songs, "Yalifu," which, when translated, says, "Pelican, lend me your wings."

The Whole Story

Elsewhere in New York City, Janka Nabay landed, like so many immigrants, displaced from his home country of Sierra Leone because of civil war. A self-made star in his home country, he's known as the "Bubu King" for taking bubu music — a traditional Muslim processional music that the Temne people of Northwestern Sierra Leone played only during the month of Ramadan — and turning it into a contemporary, danceable genre. Back home, Nabay gained fame by dubbing and selling his own tapes around the capital city of Freetown and elsewhere and playing raucous live shows.

Since arriving in the United States ten years ago, he's found that being the Bubu King means much less over here. In fact, he's found that most Americans know little to nothing about Sierra Leone. "I don't understand this," he exclaims. "You're talking about Black History Month, and you leave out the names 'Freetown' and 'Liberia'" — a city

and a country, respectively, populated largely by descendants of freed slaves who were sent back to Africa by well-meaning but geographically un-derinformed abolitionists in the early 1800s. "How can you call this black history?" he asks. "You're leaving out half the story if you leave out Africa!"

Part of Americans' deficit of knowledge about Sierra Leone, Nabay believes, is because Sierra Leone suffers from something of a cultural branding problem. "When you hear reggae music," he offers as an example, "where do you think [of]? Jamaica! I want my bubu music to be the signature for Sierra Leone. Everybody in Sierra Leone knows bubu." Of course, getting the rest of the world clued in to the sound of Sierra Leone is easier said than done.

One of the biggest barriers to the rise of bubu music in the States — as is true of many styles immigrants bring with them — is financial. Nabay's story is similar to that of many musicians who find themselves in immigrant enclaves in less-wealthy areas of large American cities. "The clubs in our neighborhoods [in the outer boroughs of New York City], they hold only 70 people, maybe 100," Nabay explains. "And every night, you have four bands. You see where I am going with this?"

Economy of scale works in reverse in this setting, and musicians simply can't make a living if they're taking home $30 a night. Meanwhile, in the interest of their bottom lines, the larger clubs that are found in the swankier neigh-borhoods of New York — and Los Angeles and Chicago and so on — seldom book international artists who are unknown to American crowds. Given the limitations of those two options, it quickly becomes an economic impossibility for most musicians who immigrate to perform full-time.

Nabay, not one to be dissuaded, spent most days working in restaurant kitchens and food trucks and played what gigs he could at night when he first

arrived. He'd cobble together bands of fellow Africans or play along with recorded tracks. One night at a Brooklyn gig, he met Syrian-American indie rocker and global music wunderkind Boshra AlSaadi, who became his first true American student. She learned his

bubu music easily, he says, and they formed a band. He explains that it was no trouble to teach his bandmates his music, largely because their background is so diverse and he believes in the universality of music. "Music has no boundaries," he says. "When the music is good, you know. They just feel my music!" Their spring 2017 release, *Build Music,* is their second album as a band.

Nabay also believes in music's direct and universal power as a change agent, even if the music itself is not overtly political, and that this is particularly characteristic of the powerfully upbeat genre of bubu. "I'm trying to play this music in the White House," he explains, fully aware of the difficulty of taking Muslim music to a White House that has been openly hostile to Muslim communities. "Oh yes," he exclaims,

Aurelio

Ani Cordero

talking of the president. "If he hears my music right now, he'll love it. If he wants me to go play my bubu music that originated from my Muslim background in the White House, yes! I will go! Right away! He is the president! It is a great honor, and he will love it."

Tearing Down Walls

Even as Janka Nabay exudes unabashed hope about speaking truth directly to power with music, other artists are using music to foment change from the bottom up.

Singer, songwriter, and multi-instrumentalist Ani Cordero approaches her music with an eye toward social justice, with immigration as a main motif alongside environmental justice, feminism, racial justice, and government corruption. Born stateside in a musical Puerto Rican family (both parents were *tuna* musicians, a collegiate folkloric genre found throughout the Spanish-speaking world), neither Cordero nor her family are immigrants. Puerto Rico is an unincorporated territory of the United States, though Cordero explains that "colony" is a better contemporary description. Nonetheless, she sees Latin America as many pieces of a larger story. "I may not be an immigrant myself," she explains, "but that doesn't mean that I don't heavily sympathize. And these are my people too. Latin America is many countries, but among us, there is a solidarity."

In an era of wall-building and ICE raids that specifically target Hispanic communities, Cordero finds that as a human, as a woman, and as a mother, she cannot remain silent. "Can you imagine," she asks, "sending your 10-year-old across the border by themselves because they're safer crossing the border than staying with you? The lack of empathy and understanding [among non-immigrants] is incomprehensible to me."

Cordero's music hits hard on these issues, but never loses an element of hope. "Voy Caminando" ("I'm Walking"), for example, from her album *Querido Mundo*, released last spring, speaks about the forced journey that so many take, but also about the need to remain positive and find within ourselves "the hope that propels us to new futures and new places."

"My mission with *Querido Mundo*," she says, "is to go into any community I can and try to get them more involved in activism, using the music as a platform."

Cordero explains that she and her band work somewhat as modular units, and can play full shows for dance parties or studious, sit-down crowds, but she can also snag her guitar and her accordion player, a neighbor in her Brooklyn 'hood, jump on the subway, and head down to the local cultural center or to a church basement and do shows easily.

BEK ANDERSEN

> **"Approaching any music that's not Western music and giving it the blanket term of 'world music' is so ignorant to music at large. It doesn't give respect to the fact that there's so much more to music than just American-style pop music."**
>
> Sinkane

This method of music-as-activism in the Latin community is not new. Where Americana fans are surely familiar with Woody Guthrie, Pete Seeger, and other artists who have used folk music as a tool for direct action, those who are familiar with contemporary Latin American history and its folk music are just as familiar with the *nueva canción* movement — a folk revivalist movement during the 1970s and '80s that was borne out of radical opposition to right-wing dictatorships (Spain's Franco, Chile's Pinochet, etc.). Singers like Mercedes Sosa (Argentina) and Gilberto Gil (Brazil) and bands like Os Mutantes (a Brazilian band with whom Cordero has played drums on tour) rose to international fame during that time, despite very real threats against their lives and freedoms.

Some artists did not survive: Chilean singer-songwriter Victor Jara was among those tortured and killed shortly after Pinochet's coup in 1973, and others went into hiding or left their countries altogether.

Cordero is a dedicated scholar of that era, its musicians and songs, and the legacies thereof, and she sees it as once again relevant in the modern political context. "We take our safety for granted ... [but] this idea that democracy is a stable thing is just not true," she says.

For all this darkness, there are still love songs on Cordero's album and in every live show. "I use my music to inspire others, to combat my own sorrow, and to come to terms with where we are and where we need to be. And sometimes that means love songs!" She laughs, adding that music and dance are a universal form of self-care. "Self-care is so important. We all need it."

Defying Categories

Is there anything more truly universal than a love song or, for that matter, a dance party? Often, when discussing African artists in the same context as Puerto Rican singer-songwriters, there's a temptation to refer to it all under the same banner of "world music," but most artists from outside of America will balk at the implications of the phrase. This is not, as some assume, because the term is too broad, but rather because it's too narrow. Sinkane, for one, is determined that his music will not end up in the "world music" category.

"Approaching any music that's not Western music and giving it the blanket term of 'world music' is so ignorant to music at large," he says. "It doesn't give respect to the fact that there's so much more to music than just American-style pop music. It's hard for people to understand it, I'm sure, just because they haven't been exposed to it, but ... that's what we're here to do."

Born Ahmed Gallab in London to Sudanese parents, but raised all over the United States (including stints in Ohio and Utah — his parents are professors and moved fairly often), it's no surprise that Sinkane's music doesn't fit tidily into any singular category. It employs Sudanese rhythms and funk horns, '70s soul-style falsetto vocals, and reverby, prog-rock-y compositions. The band's members are from all over the world — "We look like a United Colors of Benetton ad," Sinkane jokes, but as far as backgrounds and musical influences, "it's really what we call 'celestial diversity.' It represents the United States and the world at large."

Still, the contemporary nature of the band's sound is far from contrived. They make no direct effort to appeal to any one group, whether people from a specific country or belief system or fans of a specific kind of music. Sinkane, like every other musician mentioned here, believes in the universality of music. "Ultimately, the bigger picture for me isn't the sounds, but the way we all relate; the universal nature of it all," he says. "I mean, look at the relationship between reggae and country: the statement, the energy. [Both of those styles are] coming from people who feel the same way about things in their lives."

Indeed, the stories of these four artists are a few among thousands, even millions: musicians performing for, with, and about their people. They pick up both old instruments and new ones, traditional songs and ultra-contemporary ones. For all we, as humans, feel the need to put labels on things, the universal story of these artists — as well as those who came before them and those who will come after — is not in the unique sounds, though that certainly makes them fun and identifiable. It's in the messages that are true for everyone.

The sounds are a vehicle for this message. On Sinkane's newest album, *Life and Livin' It,* the dominant message is positive, but not relentlessly. His music seeks to encourage listeners to question everything, even as it tries to help folks make it through every day, even the hard ones, with some element of optimism intact. As he sings in "U'huh," a nod at Kendrick Lamar's "Alright," which became an anthem of the Black Lives Matter movement: "As long as we try, we're gonna be all right." ∎

Calan

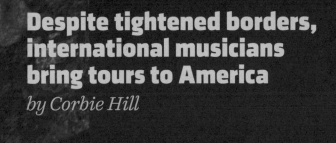

SOMETHING TO DECLARE

Despite tightened borders, international musicians bring tours to America

by Corbie Hill

> **"If I become a violent [person] because people use violence against me, I'm not going to gain anything. But if I insist on peace, maybe I will be able to make this world we are living in a peaceful place to live."**
>
> Albert Mazibuko (Ladysmith Black Mambazo)

N SEPTEMBER 2015, PATRICK Rimes and Sam Humphreys of traditional Welsh folk band Calan landed in a Chicago holding cell, awaiting a flight back to the United Kingdom along with others who had been denied entry to the United States. Immigration officials cursed at the people in the cell and some of the other detained people were difficult and antagonistic right back. Some detainees were shoving a woman in a wheelchair, and no one seemed to care.

Humphreys and Rimes had toured in the US before, with no incident, but this time they were taken for questioning when they arrived, then left to sit, waiting, for several hours before learning they wouldn't be let into the country. They were searched with demeaning thoroughness. "At one point, the guy who was searching Sam said, 'What have you got in your trousers? What's that?'" recalls Calan manager Huw Williams. "And Sam said, 'They're my balls.' That's how personal the search was."

Rimes and Humphreys felt as though they were being treated like criminals. They had to hand over their phones, belts, and shoes and were kept in the holding cell overnight. The next day, they were driven to the airport in a caged van. They had to stand in line and watch all the other passengers board, and their passports weren't returned to them until the plane was off the ground, bound for the UK.

They were told they were "refused entry to the United States without prejudice," says Williams, noting that that's different from being banned. To make things right, they could go home, get visas, and come back. The problem was that they already had visas: they'd paid for them months earlier, long before the US leg of their 2015 tour. But a worldwide glitch in the American computer system kept their visas from printing. Instead, immigration officials gave them stamps, which they were told would work the same as visas. They used those stamps to enter the United States twice before, in late 2015. It was the third time they returned when they were singled out, thrown in a holding cell, and eventually sent back to Wales.

Ever since, they can't use streamlined systems like ESTA (the Electronic System for Travel Authorization), even if they're just traveling for fun, explains Williams, "because this computer-generated system will ask the question, 'Have you ever been turned away from the United States?' And they have to say yes, which means they can never go to the United States unless they have a visa."

"It's like they're automatically suspicious of what you're doing," he adds. "You have to make sure you have the paperwork, because one glitch [and] you're on the plane, you're home."

Fellow Welsh singer Kizzy Crawford experienced something similar earlier the same year, while en route to the Folk Alliance International conference in Kansas City. She flew from London to Toronto and was allowed through US immigration just fine there. When her connecting flight to Kansas City was canceled, she left the airport to stay overnight at a hotel. When she returned to catch her rescheduled flight the next morning, she was pulled aside, peppered with questions, and taken to secondary questioning, where she broke down.

"I didn't know why I was being taken for questioning," she told *Wales Online*'s David Owens. "I didn't know where I was." Crawford, who was only 18 at the time, was terrified. The more nervous, confused, and upset she got, the more antagonistic the officials were. "So they deported her on mental health grounds," Williams says.

The Old, Weird America

Once inside America's borders, things tend to get easier for a foreign traveler, and those who keep their eyes and ears open can learn a lot about the country as they move around.

In early 2016, English folksinger Billy Bragg, who has visited the United States annually since the '80s, joined American singer-songwriter Joe Henry to explore the tradition of American train songs via the railroads themselves. The pair boarded a passenger train in Chicago's Union Station and traveled south, through St. Louis and into Texas, and then west, through Arizona and finally to Los Angeles. Across nine stops, and at train stations and platforms in towns like Alpine, Texas, and Poplar Bluff, Missouri, Bragg and Henry recorded old railroad songs. They skipped the studio, instead setting up microphones wherever made the most sense and recording on the spot.

"Two guys playing guitar in a railway station is not a big deal anywhere," Bragg says. "Nobody gave us a second look." The resulting field-recorded album, *Shine a Light: Field Recordings from the Great American Railroad,* came out last September.

Riding an American passenger train showed Bragg the side of America that touring musicians don't see from what he calls the touring bubble: If you fly in or go from downtown music venue to downtown music venue via interstates,

Kizzy Crawford

you don't really see the trailer parks. Bragg has always sought the alternate route. He used to tell people that if they wanted to see real America, they should eat in a Woolworth's.

"When we first came to America in the 1980s," he says, "I felt like I was a member of a cargo cult. The best time we could have in America would be to go to a really big Kmart, because you could find shit in there that you just don't find in the UK."

Riding the train was a lot like that. He points out that the United States puts more freight on the rails than any industrialized nation, but that there's hardly a passenger rail system anymore. To a European, this is baffling. To Bragg, a student of American culture and folklore, it's also something he simply had to experience.

"It is a mythical thing," he says. "It's the only part of what Greil Marcus called the old, weird America that you can still buy a ticket for.

"You can't ride on a stagecoach anymore. You can go and dress as a cowboy and ride around Montana, but it's not really a functioning thing anymore." On this journey, Bragg felt like he was following a fossilized path, one that passed through decaying towns that once relied on the railroad. His fellow passengers, too, stuck in his mind. Most were people who couldn't fly for whatever reason — health, money, paranoia.

"It's a different part of America that you see as well, because you're very often snaking around, going through towns and cities, and you have to stop to cross active roads," Bragg says. "So you might be sitting on a train ... and you're looking into someone's backyard, almost into the back windows of their house. That's an America I've not seen before, despite coming to your country since 1984."

"I know Americans," he explains. "I speak to Americans all the time, I read newspapers in America, I ride public transport in America." Earlier this year, Bragg returned yet again, to Kansas City for the 2017 Folk Alliance International conference, where he was the keynote speaker. He got into the country fine — in fact, new visa-scanning machines at Dallas/Fort Worth International Airport made it an easier process than usual, he says — yet he knows the United States isn't friendly and welcoming to everyone.

"I see what an amazing, vibrant place it is," he says. "[And] I see what a crazy, dangerous place it can be, like anywhere."

A New Sheriff in Town

Though Crawford and the members of Calan had regrettable experiences at the border during the Obama era, a renewed interest in border security under President Trump has brought fresh eyes to how international travelers enter the United States — something many Americans likely didn't consider very frequently until now. Under the new administration's aggressive stance on immigration, travel to and from a number of predominantly Muslim countries has been banned and there are plans to line the US/Mexico border

(much of which is already fenced) with a wall. Nonetheless, international musicians keep coming. Many of them note, once you're inside, everyday people are as gracious and welcoming as they've ever been. It's at the border — where some get the impression that officials can arbitrarily detain travelers and bar them entry — that traveling to the United States as a touring musician has become increasingly tense.

"It's as if you're entering the Soviet Union in 1964," notes Calan manager Williams.

Albert Mazibuko can chart 30 years in border policy changes, having toured the United States since the mid-'80s with celebrated South African a cappella ensemble Ladysmith Black Mambazo. Though mainstream American audiences were exposed to Ladysmith via Paul Simon's *Graceland*, which prominently featured its rich choral harmonies, the group dates to the mid-'60s, with Mazibuko's own involvement starting in 1969. Ladysmith has maintained a message of peace, love, and harmony throughout apartheid and the extreme civil unrest that gripped South Africa when that system of racial segregation finally fell; members of Ladysmith have died violently, yet the ensemble consistently takes the high road when responding to injustice. Nelson Mandela commended their dedication to peace and harmony, declaring the group South Africa's cultural ambassadors.

"If I become a violent [person] because people use violence against me, I'm not going to gain anything," Mazibuko says from a Florida hotel room. "But if I insist on peace, maybe I will be able to make this world we are living in a peaceful place to live."

While Mazibuko says American audiences and everyday people have always been very nice to his band, the Trump era has brought a change. "Some of them [in the audience], they come to us and they cry," he says. "We can see tears from the older people. They say, 'Wow. We are sorry that what is happening in our country.' Then we say

to them, 'Keep being strong.'"

As a frequent international traveler and a person who has lived in a number of countries, author Mohsin Hamid has experienced several periods of US border policy. As a Pakistani citizen, he has experienced the extra level of screening people from Muslim countries take as a given in American airports.

"Post-September 11, there was a time I used to get sent for secondary inspection whenever I came into America," says Hamid. "I was always selected for special security checks when I was boarding flights. I was once pulled off a flight in North Carolina because they had forgotten to do the special security check," he says, laughing as he adds, "A trainee was on duty."

As an author, he travels as often as a touring musician would; in early 2017, he appeared at bookstores in the UK and US in support of *Exit West*, a novel about two refugees' struggle to survive in a fictionalized, near-future migrant crisis. He's a widely published journalist and essayist, too, which has afforded him remarkable access to the people who make foreign policy decisions.

"I think I was giving a lecture at the State Department and I said, 'Look — the consul general of the United States has been over to my house many times for dinner and felt perfectly safe in Lahore, in Pakistan. I'm here giving a talk to you at the State Department, so you guys really don't think I'm a threat, obviously, if these things are happening,'" Hamid explains over the phone from Manchester, England. "'Yet I'm constantly having extra searches and extra questioning. It means either you do think I'm a threat, in which case why are you risking yourselves exposing yourselves to me, or you don't, in which case, you can't be bothered taking me off some list?'"

He adds that the post-September 11 screenings have softened with time, yet he feels the whole tenor of the Trump administration could make travel to the US tougher than it was back then. It was

> **"They say Welsh and English people are polite. You don't get any more polite, I think, than an American. No one says, 'Hello, good afternoon,' when they get into a lift over here, but they will in America. They won't ignore each other. That's why it's worth going."**
> Huw Williams

a hassle, Hamid admits, being stopped and questioned before boarding a plane, but he felt the people at the top of the chain were trustworthy.

"I don't necessarily agree with this process, but I expect that it'll be done in the proper way," he says of the changes that came after the September 11 attacks. "I don't know if that's still the case. Is there now more of a sense of, 'Who cares? Let's just be arbitrarily not nice to people'?

"If, from the top down, the message that's coming down isn't that we think people are equal and we believe in decency, then isn't it possible that people lower down the chain will behave more badly? And that's the frightening part of what the administration is like now."

Similarly, Huw Williams wonders aloud if it's still safe for non-American artists to tour in the United States. Calan's American agent reassures him that it's perfectly safe, but Williams can't help but wonder: It's "a real dumbass question," he says, but one he felt he had to ask.

"It might be the case that we are just getting all the bad news," he says. "That's all we [hear about], is policemen shooting innocent people, assaulting innocent people, Donald Trump banning people from seven countries. It's becoming frightening."

He mentions a conversation he had with an American who was visiting the United Kingdom, who observed with envy that the British were not afraid of their government. "And I thought, 'Who on earth is afraid of their government?'"

he says, "unless you're living in some dictatorship. If you're in a Western democracy, why are you suspicious or afraid of your government?"

Good for Business

Of course, there's plenty of reasons for artists from around the world to tour in the States, even after some of them have faced humiliation at the border. When Williams says entering the US is like entering the Soviet Union, he means it in two ways: the officials can be obstinate — rigidly, if arbitrarily, enforcing regulations, miring travelers in red tape — but also, once you're inside the country, the everyday people are gracious and easygoing.

"They say Welsh and English people are polite," Williams says. "You don't get any more polite, I think, than an American. No one says, 'Hello, good afternoon,' when they get into a lift over here, but they will in America. They won't ignore each other. That's why it's worth going. That might be because we tend to talk to liberal, left-wing folkies, maybe. I don't know, but they're the nicest people on earth."

Such good-natured charm by itself, though, isn't enough to bring a band back to the US after humiliation at the border. It has to be a safe place to travel and make financial sense, too, Williams says. And there are benefits on both sides of the cultural exchange when an international act tours the United States. Williams wants to bring Welsh music to festivals in the States. Maybe people won't buy tickets just to see Calan, he

admits, but a festival that includes them could seem just a bit more interesting, just a bit more appealing with more diversity on the bill.

"It keeps the festival going," he says. "You're going to make money out of your audience; we're going to make money out of your audience."

Williams discusses touring the United States in business terms: As a manager, he's here to do business, and what he's offering is a fiery young Welsh band, one that fuses old jigs and reels with flavors tastefully borrowed from jazz, rock, and bluegrass, then blisters through them with passion and precision. And when those polite American audiences show their appreciation, it's often with their credit cards in hand. After learning about Rimes and Humphreys' problems at the border, fans in the States paid extra for CDs just to help them recoup losses from canceled gigs and extra flights. Calan was able to make money on that tour, but not as much as they should have because of all the extra expenses incurred from their visa debacle.

"There will always be technical [and] paperwork issues, and I always approach the border anticipating that there is going to be some sort of issue," says Aengus Finnan. "I am always pleasantly surprised when there is no issue at all."

Finnan was born in Ireland and grew up in Canada, though these days he's based in Kansas City, where he is executive director of Folk Alliance International. In his touring musician past, he experienced international travel

Tinariwen

like Bragg, Mazibuko, the members of Calan, or anyone who's crossed a border for business or work. But with Folk Alliance International, which invites musicians and other attendees from all corners of the globe for its annual conference, Finnan's perspective has broadened. Folk Alliance gives musicians traveling to the US as much useful information as possible, with the aim of minimizing confusion — and possible refusal — at the border.

"If you're going into a foreign country, they're going to ask, where are you staying? What are the dates?" Finnan explains. "Once you start to fumble with things, it raises suspicion for whoever the border patrol officer is."

So Folk Alliance makes sure artists and delegates know what documents they'll need and what the immigration process is. They remind artists to have their itinerary written down, including how many days they'll be in the country and the address of their hotel. The organization provides letters to conference attendees that explain the

nature of their trip, all on Folk Alliance International letterhead, and artists and delegates are told to keep this paper in hand. When border officials ask a question, Finnan counsels them, avoid extraneous detail and keep your answers to the point.

"The reality is, there is a process for each country to vet access to that country," he says. And, he points out, officials have to follow that process. There's the capacity for human and computer error, sure, but border officers are trained to be stern and diligent.

"I am also not putting the responsibility on the artist, either. It's a collective responsibility," Finnan says, meaning both the person trying to enter a country and the border official need to be present and attentive to the process. "It's not as simple as demonizing border security because they don't want to admit someone through. There are all sorts of elements that go in."

Among the issues that do need to be worked through, Finnan says, are things like processing time for visas and

reciprocity. It's easier for a US artist to enter Canada than for a Canadian artist to enter the US, for instance.

While it's not directly related to border policies, Finnan says, some artists expressed concerns about traveling to the United States for the Folk Alliance conference under the Trump administration. Some canceled on political grounds, while others expressed concerns about racial profiling. These are always issues that require discussion, he admits, but in 2017 there has been an increased sense of concern. Still, he says, "Despite it all, we had an exceptional year."

For one, 2017 was the highest attended year for the Folk Alliance conference, with 21 nations represented. The theme was overtly political, with the conference celebrating activism in folk music and featuring speakers like Bragg who take on the issues of the day directly in the form of protest song. For these artists, the desire to come to the United States outweighed their concerns.

A similar sentiment emerged when I

California desert as they are in their native Sahara. That familiarity with the US is something they share with Billy Bragg and Ladysmith's Mazibuko — artists who have found great personal and professional value in touring this side of the world, despite the faults and challenges.

Importing a Message

It was a warm and blustery March evening in Durham, North Carolina, as severe thunderstorms swept through. Wind, hail, and torrential rain pummeled the city, but inside the Carolina Theatre it was serene and warm.

Ladysmith Black Mambazo's audience was the kind of crowd Tinariwen's Abdallah Ag Alhousseyni looks forward to encountering in the United States: it was ethnically diverse, outfits ran the gamut from top-of-the-line evening wear to T-shirts and jeans, and attendants ranged in age from preschool children to white-haired folks with walkers.

Ladysmith introduced "Long Walk to Freedom" with the proud announcement that South Africa has been a democracy for 22 years, and the audience cheered. Indeed, struggles for civil rights and equality came up several times that evening, but were presented positively every time: Rather than focusing on strife, Ladysmith focused on the act of overcoming it; they focused on the victories.

"If you have a positive message, that music is going to make a huge difference," Mazibuko asserts. "[You might say], 'Oh, maybe there will be a few people.' No — it's going to make a lot of difference."

For five-plus decades, positivity and hope have been conscious hallmarks of Ladysmith Black Mambazo, and Mazibuko hopes the choir will spread that message indefinitely. Two generations made up the choir on the 2017 tour, with a third generation waiting in the figurative wings. This youngest singer has toured with Ladysmith once, but he had to return to school. The choir will be there for him when he's ready.

"This music, it shouldn't die if we pass on," Mazibuko says.

spoke recently with members of Malian Tuareg band Tinariwen. "Obviously the sociopolitical context is a little difficult right now, but it won't affect our determination" to tour in the States, says the group's guitarist and singer Abdallah Ag Alhousseyni.

He adds, through a translator, that Tinariwen has never had issues getting into the US, and he likes the diversity of American audiences. He sees a variety of ages and social groups in the audience when Tinariwen plays the States.

"Tour buses are always better in the US — very comfortable," Ag Alhousseyni says. "When you're on the road for several weeks, it really makes a difference."

The desert nomads recorded their most recent album, *Elwan* (which translates to "The Elephants"), at Rancho de la Luna Studios in Joshua Tree, California, during a four-day break in the band's 2014 tour. Tinariwen has traveled the US many times, with some members living in the Southwest for a time, so they were as at home in the

Indeed, one of music's strengths is that it can communicate across generations, or across cultures, and this is another reason artists take their songs across borders. Friendly audiences and business opportunities, as exist in the US, are a draw, sure, but the intangible connection music can bring is an important piece of this puzzle. *Elwan*, the latest Tinariwen album, is about transmission, says Ag Alhousseyni — it's about methods of communication that circumvent language and culture.

"In Maghreb [the north and northwestern edge of Africa, west of Egypt], where the Tamasheq language is not understood, many children make our songs their own by inventing lyrics in Arab[ic]," Ag Alhousseyni says. "We discovered that when we recorded in [the village of] M'hamid in Morocco, where we met those fantastic children." The band encouraged these youths from the other side of the Sahara and featured them in the "Sastanàqqàm" music video. Touring, whether to desert oases or across oceans, transmits the spirit of Tinariwen's nomadic Tuareg culture away from the sands of home.

And for Ladysmith Black Mambazo, the message they brought to the US this tour was one of hope — an intangible connection, certainly, but a purposeful one. "We are told the songs that have helped in South Africa when people were divided and killing each other; these are the songs that we're singing [on this tour] because we're trying to convey our prayers to the people and to God Almighty," says Mazibuko. "Help this country in this lifetime."

Yet to get to that point — to enter the US to play music professionally, to get to know the everyday people, or to connect with audiences on that intangible, almost spiritual level that's specific to live music, international artists must first make it across the border. And the US border — like any border, as Aengus Finnan points out, as every nation has them — is a threshold where human error, red tape, or computer glitches can scuttle even the noblest or most talented musicians' plans.

"That's the system, it seems to me. This is the law, and this is what they stick to," says Huw Williams. "There doesn't seem to be any leeway." ∎

Cuba's Heartbeat

Words and photographs by Jill Kettles

n Cuba, music is the language of survival, hope, and love. Wherever you stand, walk, or eat, you're likely to find music. It's inseparable from Cuba's culture, the glue that holds its heart and soul together. This past spring, I spent a week in Cuba, exploring the island nation's culture and music, photographing street musicians and concerts for *No Depression*.

In Hamel Alley in Havana, I observed a group of women rehearsing a rumba — they told stories in their native tongue, chanting for easy memorization. I heard the contemporary music of the band Tumbao Habana at the Casa de la Musica, where the crowd danced late into the night.

I heard classic Latin songs like "20 Años" and "Guantanamera" set to salsa and jazz piano. I heard the sad, romantic vibrato of Buena Vista Social Club, whose music has moved people for more than 30 years. I heard the simple nylon-stringed guitar of an old man tenderly, shyly sharing his magic with me through a barred doorway. I even heard Kool & the Gang's 1980s hit "Celebration" blaring from a man's boombox.

Buskers were everywhere — on corners, in restaurants and bars, entertaining tourists and natives alike, collecting tips. No matter where I went, the music had an underlying rhythm that made me want to move. What's more, it seemed that everyone knew how to play an instrument and sing, and those who didn't listened to the music others have made, loudly, in their cars, at dinner, in their pedal taxis, and on the boomboxes carried on their shoulders as they serenaded the American girl with the camera.

KEEPING A TETHER

Richard Shindell's American music takes on new flavor in Argentina

by Kim Ruehl

SEVENTEEN YEARS AGO, lifelong New Yorker Richard Shindell's wife was offered a teaching job in her home country of Argentina. For Shindell, the decision to move required little hesitation — as a singer-songwriter whose career has been made traveling gig to gig, it barely mattered whether his home base was a train ride away from midtown Manhattan or a short drive from Buenos Aires. So, they loaded up the kids and moved on down.

Nearly two decades and eight albums later, Shindell has become accustomed to the rhythm of life as an expat musician. Except for his 2004 release *Vuelta*, on which he dabbled in Argentine styles, collaborated with Argentine musicians, and sang a smidge of Spanish, his music has yet to completely go native. "Musically speaking, I'm not very adventurous," he admits. "I haven't learned to play tango ... [or] chamamé or bolero. I'd feel like a poser."

Indeed, Shindell found his musical voice long ago, and it is thick with first- and third-person stories, parables about life and how to surmount its troubles. And there's something decidedly American about it.

In the fall of 2015, he joined singer-songwriter Lucy Kaplansky onstage at Nashville's City Winery for a set of tunes during AmericanaFest. The pair called their collaboration the Pine Hill Project, though fans would be forgiven for seeing it as a reprisal of their Cry Cry Cry effort from 1998, when Dar Williams rounded them out to a trio. But that little folk supergroup happened before the turn of the century, before Shindell and his family expatriated. It was quite literally another time and place. Seeing him onstage during AmericanaFest, next to his old friend and collaborator, I noticed an exquisite creative tension between their near-familial comfort with one another and the way distance — geographic, cultural, personal — separates people.

One morning a year or so later, as the rain fell where I was in lower Appalachia, Shindell sat in his car, in the sun, somewhere near San Miguel del Monte, Argentina, and tried to explain what it's like to navigate that tension, what it's like to move to another country.

"You're never quite where you are," he said. "You're never at home, even though you're at home, it's never quite the same. You're always a little bit removed or not quite comfortable. That position could be very interesting from a writing point of view or a psychological point of view, but it can also be a cross to bear. I think a lot of people who have left their countries — whether the United States or any other place — feel something like that. So my records, in one way or another, are [my way of] trying to get back — not literally, but in a psychological way. To keep the tether, culturally and emotionally.

"It's a very, very intense thing being an expat," he adds after a breath. "A lot of people think it's like, 'Oh, you left and went to someplace sunnier.' No, no, no. A lot of people think I left because I didn't like George [W.] Bush, but no. I left before that happened. When I left, it was a whole different political situation. In other words, people project onto my expat status all kinds of things that just aren't true, and it can be a little bit frustrating. ... There are upsides too. It's beautiful here and we have a wonderful life. It turned out to be the right thing for my family. We've raised our kids here. ... But, there's a psychological thing going on which is constantly in my songs, one way or another."

That psychological thing was on fullest display on *Vuelta*, through which he explored Argentine themes and instrumental sounds. It opened him up to a collaboration with Argentine fusion outfit Puente Celeste, whom he cites as one of his great musical loves in his assumed home. But for all the conscious attempt to make an album that might root him in a land that was then so new to him — even as it is one of the oldest places on

"You're never quite where you are. You're never at home, even though you're at home, it's never quite the same. You're always a little bit removed or not quite comfortable. That position could be very interesting from a writing point of view or a psychological point of view, but it can also be a cross to bear."

Richard Shindell

Earth — the songs still sounded like your standard Richard Shindell tunes: stories about heartbroken people who search for meaning, connection, hope, and love. These universal themes are replete in his work, and have been the threads tying together his entire career. Whether that can be attributed to his empathic nature as an artist or to his personal life story is probably rich fodder for analysts. But Shindell recognizes the intrigue in the fact that the bookends of his life thus far have been rooted in Latin America.

"I lived in Chile for a year when I was a very small boy — four years old," he says. "My earliest memories were living in Latin America. They tell me I spoke very good Spanish then. I proceeded to forget it all when we moved back to the United States and I had to relearn it. But I went to a neighborhood day care center when I was four, and a Chile kindergarten, and hung out with my little Chilean friends. So there's a connection with me and Latin America that goes way back. Raising my children here perhaps felt comfortable in some way."

A Similar Stew

While Shindell didn't have to do much soul searching to embrace the move, he has had to adjust to the rhythms of a different culture. He refers to these as internalized, agreed-upon "codes" — how to be when one enters a café, what one does while waiting in line, how one makes one's way along crowded city sidewalks. That said, Buenos Aires is quite like Shindell's native New York, and not just because big cosmopolitan cities all over

the world share basic realities like congestion, diversity, noise, and traffic.

"When I first got to Buenos Aires, I thought, 'These people look like New Yorkers. This looks like New York.' Except that they were speaking Spanish," he explains. "When emigration from Europe was happening and people were getting on boats and going to New York – from Italy, from the Ukraine, from Germany, from wherever — all of those people ... had brothers or sisters who decided to get on the other boat for Buenos Aires. At that time, Argentina was a very wealthy country — one of the wealthiest countries in the world — underpopulated, great land, beautiful scenery, great climate. So one brother got on the boat to New York and the other brother got on the boat to Buenos Aires, and they never saw each other again."

And while we know well that the New York brother in this scenario docked in a city where Italian music was mingling with Irish, Jewish, and African styles, a similar stew was brewing in Buenos Aires.

"Argentina [is] a melting pot of different kinds of immigrants, a particular blend of influences," explains Puente Celeste percussionist Santiago Vazquez. "That special way in which those entrances were melted [together with] traditions in Argentina is [what became known as] tango, chamamé, chacarera, and others. ... Even though there's not much African descendants living in Argentina, [that music] has made its impact. Also, of course, European music with European harmonies. Indian people have some influence on it too, as well as German influences like bandoneon or

accordion."

Vazquez knows that of which he speaks. A versatile shape-shifter of a percussionist, his band incorporates most of the musical styles he mentioned into its innovative sound, which is so broad in style and influence it would come across almost American if it weren't so entirely Argentinian.

"At first," he notes, "Puente Celeste started as my own personal project in which I could play all kinds of original compositions without boundaries of styles. Later, I started to call [in] some musicians that were bringing their own compositions, with their own influences. [We] slowly configured a very specific-sounding group, in which all the influences of the five members were present, trying not to avoid any influence but also trying not to push any influence or do any kind of artificial fusion. With time, the group got a very particular style that has been of some influence for new groups in Argentina in these last years."

The "Puente" part of his band's name translates as "bridge" ("Celeste" means "blue sky") and, as he says, its music bridges not only cultural traditions but stylistic elements as well. There's no comfortable category for describing it, aside from calling it "music" — or, as Shindell describes it, "completely free."

On "Otra Vez el Mar" from their 2009 release *Canciones*, a jazz harmonica swings against windswept keys and Vazquez's whimsical, soundtrack-of-life percussion. The opening of their *Mañana Domingo* album trots along on the tails of a flute, played to artistry by Marcelo Mogilevski, whom Shindell likens to the

Puente Celeste

Chris Thile of Argentine woodwinds — and steady rhythm guitar. Its vocals are smooth and flight-like, a bird flying straight on a breeze, occasionally kicked up or bucked down from a rough patch of air. It could almost be some strange brand of freeform rap if not for the infusions of melody. You can hear the influence of all these things (and Mogilevski's flute) pouring through on Shindell's "Fenario" (from *Vuelta*), though its structure has the verse-chorus-verse pattern typical of American folk and its tone is a bit darker. The influence comes through, too, on last year's *Careless*, whose title track employs Shindell's rhythmic, melodic speaking voice, which plods along until it catches air on the refrain: "I've learned to live with it now," he sings — a line that can only feel careless when paired with such a melody.

Whether or not Shindell borrowed these musical ideas from Puente Celeste is hard to say — artistic influences are so baked into the unconscious mind that they often come through in songwriting without the writer having much say. But

these are the subtle things that pass back and forth when musicians spend enough time with each other's creations, the same way one language might begin to employ the words of another — liaison, alarm, macho, biscuit — without losing its own identity.

Everyday Music

One might expect so much cross-pollination in a cosmopolitan city the size of Buenos Aires, but an hour or two away, where Shindell now lives, near San Miguel del Monte, things move a little more slowly. "It's like Nebraska or Iowa," he says. "It's very agricultural. This is the nearest town to where we are. Out where we are, there's barely any [cell phone] signal at all, so I come into town whenever I need to do anything that requires a signal. But even in town, the technology is about 15 years behind [the US]."

While most music culture in Buenos Aires is similar to that of American cities in that people experience music by

consuming it at concerts or by downloading albums, both Vazquez and Shindell note that rural areas of Argentina employ music as a matter of daily life. Shindell references the tango bands that pop up not to give a performance but to facilitate the communal qualities of a dance. He also name-checks Missiones-based, renowned accordionist Chango Spasiuk, who descended from Ukrainian immigrants and carries on what Shindell calls "that harmonic sensibility on the accordion that was [passed down from] generations ago when his family came here." Spasiuk is as adept at klezmer as he is at chamamé, for which he's best known.

And while Shindell is quick to point out that there's nowhere with a music world as large, diverse, vibrant, and central-to-daily-life as that in the United States, there's something to be said for the breadth and depth of music culture that swirls and soars in a nation one-quarter the size of the US. For an expat like Shindell, one might imagine it feels like crossing the world and coming home. ∎

TWEAKING TRADITION

Using technology and invented instruments, Lau shape a sound all their own

by Stacy Chandler

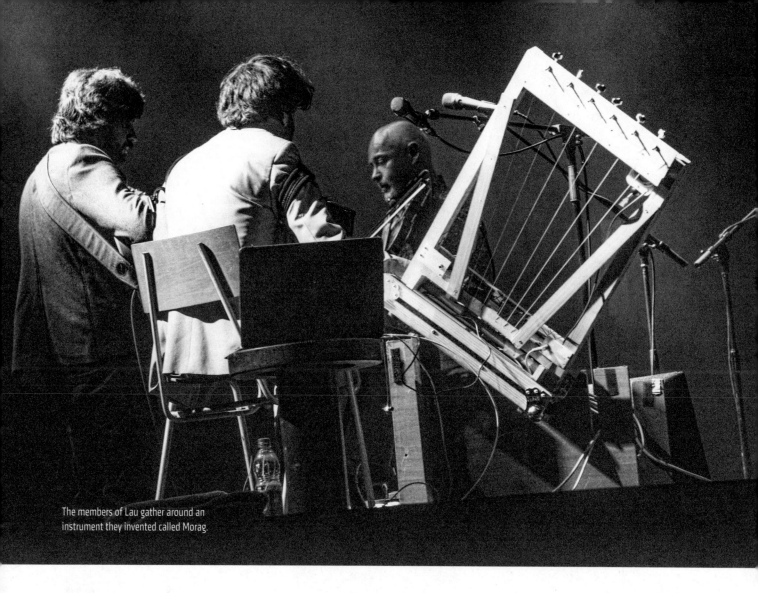

The members of Lau gather around an instrument they invented called Morag.

PUT SIMPLY, "LAU" IS A word from Scotland's Orkney Islands that means "natural light." But Kris Drever, himself from Orkney and the singer and guitarist for the Edinburgh-based band Lau, says the word is much more "multipurpose" than that.

"Like a fire when it's really blazing would be said to be 'lauing,'" he explains. Or, used another way, "to shed lau on a situation."

The situation with Lau, the band, is this: They're a trio whose music pulls from various folk traditions. They've become well-known in Scotland and far beyond over the past decade for blending those traditions with modern sounds to make something entirely new. All this has won them recognition from the BBC Radio 2 Folk Awards, among others. What's more, the band — Drever, fiddle player Aidan O'Rourke, and accordionist, keyboardist, and everything-else-ist

Martin Green — has been together for 10 solid years, even as each stays busy with solo projects and work with other artists along the way.

"We genuinely do like each other," Drever explains. "It doesn't happen that often. Musicians go from not knowing each other at all to spending lots and lots of time together. If you were in any other line of work and you spent that amount of time with your work colleagues, you'd probably want to kill one or two of them, you know. I think that we were fortunate in that we had developed fairly firm friendships before we decided to go into writing music together, and all that."

Each member of Lau pulls his weight and then some. The trio creates songs together, meeting in their practice space and engaging in "just lots and lots of trying everything," Drever says. "We've got a damp little basement, a storage area in Edinburgh, and we like to go there when it's really cold, wear lots of clothes."

He adds that teamwork also plays into

the trio's longevity. "It's a shared investment. It's not like someone's coming with songs and then we're backing them up. I don't think anybody feels they're undervalued."

The members of Lau come from different musical traditions — Drever was raised in Orkney and is the son of Orcadian folk musician Ivan Drever, O'Rourke grew up in the west coast town of Oban and was steeped in both Irish and Highland fiddle traditions, and Green grew up in Cambridge, England, with a father who played concertina and other instruments and participated in traditional Morris dances.

But even with all those differences, there is plenty the lads (as they call each other) of Lau have in common.

"There's some common languages over here," Drever says, "so although you've got people from Scotland, Ireland, England, Wales, even going into Western Europe, actually Irish traditional music is kind of a lingua franca. Even if everybody

"Although you've got people from Scotland, Ireland, England, Wales, even going into Western Europe, actually Irish traditional music is kind of a lingua franca. Even if everybody has different styles, most people have a passable repertoire of traditional Irish tunes."

Kris Drever

has different styles, most people have a passable repertoire of traditional Irish tunes. We all had that in common at least, plus an interest in Scandinavian folk music."

Lau also takes inspiration from Scottish folk artists such as the Easy Club, Ian Carr, Karen Tweed, and Anglo-Swedish fusion band Swåp, and are always going to shows together to discover new sounds.

"We all go watch gigs, and one of the things that we all identify as a good start to a good concert is when everything sounds good," Drever says. "A lot of that is ... thinking about, especially with acoustic instruments, how you make them sound good. What you need to use in order to get that acoustic instrument to sound nice and accurately, like the instrument that it is, through a bigger set of speakers."

For Lau's own music, their thoughts on sound engineering started with the basics: how to make acoustic instruments fill bigger spaces and still sound true to themselves. At some point, Green experimented with dropping the left hand of his accordion down a couple of octaves using a Roland pedal. It worked – and it also planted a seed that grew into the experimentation and acoustic-electric fusion for which Lau has become known.

"It gave us an extra dimension without being in any way disingenuous," Drever said of that first pedal. "We were able then to move in some other little bits of tinkering around with sonics. And because we introduced them a piece at a time, it never felt unnatural to us."

He continues, with a laugh: "That was the start of it, and then more stuff kept being added, to where we need a big splitter van and 23 channels or whatever it is."

Instrument Inventions

As they got bolder in their electronic experimentation, and hungrier to bring the sounds they heard in their heads to reality, existing tools didn't always fit the bill. Lau just made their own.

A creation that came to be called the Sporkatron started life as forks and spoons that Green stuck into the cardboard from a case of Carlsburg Export. The cutlery was wired into a laptop, with bottlecaps serving as control knobs. The device (which eventually was given a wooden frame and outfitted with lights and real control knobs) emits an otherworldly metallic sound when the cutlery is tapped, and can also be set to play pre-recorded samples assigned to each piece.

A more recent invention is the Morag, which Drever fondly describes by saying: "It's like a 10-year-old tried to make a harp out of balsa wood." Like most of the band's invented instruments, the idea came first, then the execution, but a name trailed behind. Morag, a somewhat old-fashioned Scottish name, was a shouted-out suggestion at a show when O'Rourke asked the audience what the band should call the thing. Like the names, the gizmos themselves evolve naturally and are

rooted in something very real.

"I am fascinated by new sound ... and electronic music offers a lot of opportunities for that, but it can also be sterile," says Green. "Anything digital is ultimately just zeros and ones, not so much sonically, but in the musician's interaction with a computer."

Green says he's drawn to the controllerism movement (originally associated with DJs) and DIY sides of music-making, "but as a traditional musician, I miss the immediacy and infinite adjustability of a 'real' instrument." So Lau's inventions are a blend of both — they're wired into a computer to trigger a sample but also can be physically played.

Much like Lau's music, their instruments are constantly evolving. According to Tim Matthew, the band's front-of-house engineer (as well as tour manager and driver) for most of their history, "Martin generally comes up with a prototype made out of cardboard and string, gets it working, and then builds a working model that we take out on the road. In a process a little like evolution, the trials of touring impose alterations on the instrument — bits get adapted, built on, reprogrammed, or discarded." Sound is paramount, of course, but portability must be considered, too.

"We try to make the Lau world something we can take anywhere," Matthew says, "and the Sporkatron was not flyable — too fragile and un-flightcase-able. Thus Morag came along, and she

mostly fits into a large pedalboard case. I have a feeling another creation will be making an appearance before too long."

Leaving the Comfort Zone

The musicians in Lau are eager to spread their passion for experimentation and blending musical traditions to other artists, near and far. In recent years they've hosted a festival called Lau-Land that's "kind of movable," Drever says, with installments in London, Bristol, Gateshead, and Edinburgh. "You can go anywhere and do it."

The idea is to bring disparate artists together and see what gets created. "We try and get people from different backgrounds together to improvise music together," Drever says. "Those things are always interesting, because everyone has a different idea even of what improvisation is. ...

"So on the one side of the room there's some fiddle players and maybe someone playing a laptop and a trumpet player, and then on the other side, [British musical improviser and filmmaker] Hugh Metcalfe, shouting swear words and hitting a drum kit with a teddy bear." He pauses to laugh. "That's kind of what it's all about. You get to have a little look into everyone's world."

Sometimes, Drever says, musicians might need a little nudge to get out of their comfort zone and try something different.

"It's a comfortable way of going outside your comfort zone," he says of the Lau-Land sessions. "But it's about learning different

approaches to music, too. It's about finding little ways through musical barriers you have yourself. You go and play with people that do something completely different, you will leave thinking about your own music differently, it's just kind of inevitable. It's very useful for all of us in that respect."

But even a band as inclined to reach out, ahead, and forward as Lau is can appreciate the value in taking a moment to look back.

On June 16, they'll release an anthology album celebrating their 10 years as a band. The songs, chosen with fan input, span Lau's four studio albums, including 2012's Tucker Martine-produced *Race the Loser* and 2015's *The Bell That Never Rang*. They'll

embark on a retrospective tour that same month, but fans know better than to expect to hear songs performed the same way they were a decade ago. Even in the span of time between finalizing an album and performing its songs onstage, the songs will always change, Drever says.

"You can kill a piece of music pretty easily by just doing it the same for 10 years. It's a guaranteed way to spoil it for everyone," he says. "It's lovely trying to think how you keep the sort of spirit of the thing while moving it on so it's interesting. We have always done that." ∎

Lau's Martin Green plays accordion
next to the Morag.

The Sunflower Bar in Belfast

TAKING IT BACK
AND GIVING IT
FORWARD

Rediscovering Belfast's traditional music

by Cara Gibney

SUMMER SOLSTICE 2014 was set against Dunluce Castle, a medieval ruin sited on a steep, treacherous outcrop overlooking the north coast of Antrim. Irish Celtic rock legends Horslips were on stage — ageless, frenetic, glorious — when they asked us to turn and watch the sun drop sluggishly into the water below.

A man whose jumper had a few beer stains on it knew every word of every song, from the first notes of the opening bars. He would run over and tell me the title and the first lines, then walk away backward, playing air drums. He was in the beer tent when the famous riff for "Trouble with a Capital T" swept off the stage. Soon enough, he ran past, pint in an outstretched fist, shouting, "I try to chase trouble but it's chasing me."

Then he fell in slow motion, the full length of him lunging forward as half a dozen of us ran toward him from different directions. His prone, still bulk landed on his thigh, his left arm slapped in front of him on the grass, his right arm determinedly pointing upwards, a third of the pint still intact in the plastic cup.

"Trouble, trouble," he mouthed. "Trouble with a capital T," we yelled as we hauled him up.

Later, he told me that where he grew up in Northern Ireland, all those years ago, you didn't listen to Irish music. Horslips were different — they were a rock band. But when it came to Irish traditional music, if you listened you kept the windows closed so nobody could hear.

Skip forward to 2017, in Maddens Bar in Belfast, where some Irish traditional music is happening upstairs in this mainstay of a pub in the center of the city. The spirits of recent history have never quite left this building — its door still has the buzzer you press before gaining entry, a hangover from the dark days when every bar needed one for security.

As Maddens fills up with a diverse crowd of Irish, British, Spanish, American, and Malaysian people, a Belfast voice at the next table leans over and asks, "Were you at the Horslips gig at Dunluce?" The man asking was one of the recovery party, and over the course of the night as the open fire glows, and the corner of the room packs slowly with more musicians and more instruments, and the reels and jigs set the tempo, we're reminded of our friend, the Horslips fan, and how important music was to him.

In the Time of the Troubles

If we hadn't gone to Maddens, we could have hit Kelly's Cellars, the Sunflower Bar, or the Duke of York to catch some live traditional music in or around downtown Belfast. The Garrick Bar is a long-standing Belfast institution known for its live music. The Five Points is new to the scene as far as traditional music is concerned, but based in a student hot spot and heaving with a new generation of listeners.

In addition to the array of venues and events in Belfast, most weeks of the year offer up at least one festival, sometimes more, including Brilliant Corners Jazz Festival, Féile an Phobail promoting Irish and international culture in the west of the city, and Féile an Earraigh on St. Patrick's Day, celebrating Irish arts and culture. Cathedral Quarter Arts Festival (CQAF) welcomes a versatile lineup of Americana and roots artists from abroad — Chip Taylor, John Murry, The Americans — as well as Irish folk from Heidi Talbot and Tír na nÓg, and traditional music mixed with pre-rock and roll from groups like Ulaid and Duke Special.

Belfast hasn't always been so vibrant, though. In the 1970s, the lights were dimmed in Northern Ireland by a devastating conflict known disingenuously as "the Troubles." The unionist/loyalist population, mostly Protestant, wanted to retain their union with the United Kingdom, while the generally Catholic republican/nationalist community looked toward the Republic of Ireland as a homeland. Although not a religious conflict, it was easy to divide Northern Ireland's citizens on religious grounds.

I was a teenager when Belfast built metal security gates around the city center to prevent bombs, and closed them early every evening. Previously busy downtown streets were empty then — it was generally accepted as too dangerous to go there. Cultural life as we had known it ceased to exist.

As the Troubles cut swaths between the communities, our identities became starker, more managed. A new normalcy set in as people carried on with their lives amid intimidation, security alerts, and a persistent threat of violence. Traditional music, previously accepted as belonging to both communities, became divisive. It was seen as associated with the Irish nationalist community, so the unionist/

Rab Cherry's box fiddle course.

Traditional music, previously accepted as belonging to both communities, became divisive. ... A generation arose that needed to keep the windows shut if they were listening to traditional music, for fear of being seen as aligning themselves with the wrong side.

loyalists tuned it out. Thus, a generation arose that needed to keep the windows shut if they were listening to traditional music, for fear of being seen as aligning themselves with the wrong side.

Now, north Belfast bears a hard legacy from a conflict that ended officially in 1998 with the Good Friday Agreement. A patchwork of small, separate communities — nationalist and loyalist areas — remain divided, some by large partitions of brick or steel, or both, known as peace walls. Today, even as the city grows, large sections of the north (and other areas) still struggle with deep divisions that often lead to, and are born from, ongoing tensions and a cycle of social deprivation.

The Duncairn Centre for Culture & Arts is based in what was once the Duncairn Presbyterian Church. Off in some side buildings, for decades, the church housed The 174 Trust. Headed by the Rev. Dr. Bill Shaw OBE, the Trust is a hard-working group that has been central to building community relations in the local area for over 30 years. Since opening the refurbished church as an arts centre in 2014, as an extension to their work through arts and culture, Duncairn Centre for Culture & Arts has provided indefatigable support for traditional music.

One thing the Centre has done to spread the music is to hold a box fiddle course taught by Rab Cherry — a Dublin-based master fiddle maker with 40 years of craft behind him. Brought up in the staunchly loyalist Sandy Row area of Belfast, he enjoyed the annual Protestant Orange parades because of his great love for pipe bands. He was also an ardent supporter of the traditionalist Irish Donegal style of fiddle playing, ultimately

co-founding Cairdeas na bhFidléirí, or Friends of the Fiddle, to help support and promote the art of fiddle-playing in the Donegal tradition.

"The pool of music that Irish musicians play, and that pipe bands play, has a massive overlap," he explains. "At the end of the day, if you aren't really into listening to music, and you don't really know very much about it, then you won't really notice that the [loyalist] flute band marching in the Orange parade or performing elsewhere is playing the same music as the people in [traditional] Irish ceilidh bands."

The folks in the Skainos Centre would agree. Run by East Belfast Mission, Skainos is an urban regeneration project in inner East Belfast. From that Centre, which sits slap-bang in the middle of loyalist/unionist Newtownards Road, they run an Irish language and music program. Irish language suffered the same fate as traditional music over the course of the conflict in Northern Ireland. Now it's difficult to convey how unlikely this language program would have been 15 years ago. How unfathomable it would have been in my teens.

"What started for us as a journey into language has become a journey into reconciliation and understanding," says language rights activist Linda Ervine, who runs the Turas program — an Irish language project aimed at reconnecting people from the Protestant community with their own history and the Irish language. "All we do is offer music and offer language. We don't give a damn about your politics, and we don't give a damn about your religion."

They also offer tin whistle classes and

Irish dance classes, and once a month they run Turn Down the Lamp, their own East Belfast traditional music session. But it was her interest in preserving the language that started Ervine, a Protestant from Newtownards Road, on the path. She wants to make the language accessible for everyone, and she wants to take away the power of people who use it for their own political ends. She sees it as something that brings people together, not something that should keep them apart.

"Thit mé i ngrá leis an teanga," she says, then translates: "I fell in love with the language."

A New Generation

All of these organizations and initiatives can happen now in Belfast because traditional Irish music has become integral to the growth and health of the city's culture, and locals don't take it for granted. A steadily growing number of visitors are helping increase demand for Irish music, but musicologist Conor Caldwell sees a slow-burn, hard-won reawakening within Belfast's inhabitants.

Caldwell is also a fiddler, tutor, and recent addition to the Belfast institution that is the Garrick Bar session on Friday evenings. To his thinking, a key element to the rise in interest is the years of work by Belfast's traditional music schools to keep the music alive. During the post-conflict era, from 1998 through the early 2000s, music schools like Andersonstown Traditional & Contemporary Music School, BelfastTrad Traditional Music & Dance Society, or Francis McPeake School of Music (no longer operating but too important to overlook) had the chance to

> **"The wide-held belief that traditional music belongs to one side? No it doesn't. It belongs where people are suffering, where people need to rise up and speak out. That's what folk music is, that's why I love it."**
>
> Ray Giffen

develop, boosted by Arts Council funding.

"You have the graduates of those schools who now understand the music and have an interest in going to a gig," says Caldwell. "It's maybe a grassroots thing but there are so many young people in the city learning traditional music seriously now."

Belfast-based uilleann piper, whistle player, composer, and producer John McSherry — one third of the trio Ulaid, who was recently nominated for a BBC Radio 2 Folk Award and who runs a session at the Sunflower Bar — believes that generating interest among young people is the key to keeping the music relevant. "It's healthy to have the purists," he says, "but you also need people to bring it forward, otherwise it's dead music. Fresh ideas make it cool for young people to play. It has to have a life, and if young people aren't interested in it, it will die."

After 20 years in the business, Pauline Scanlon, writer and vocalist of contemporary and traditional Irish music and one half of the duo Lumiere, sees signs that more young people are considering traditional Irish music as a career. Echoing McSherry, she's hopeful this infusion of youth energy will

safeguard a regular stream of fresh blood to the scene.

Originally from the Corca Dhuibhne Gaeltacht — where locals' first language is Irish — in County Kerry, in southwest Ireland, Scanlon is now based in Belfast. She voted for the first time in Northern Ireland's recent tumultuous elections and says she thrives in the creative, edgy atmosphere here. She remembers feeling a hunger for Belfast's culture and language when she first started playing here all those years ago. The mix of political thinking, social activism, creativity, and motivation creates an atmosphere that Scanlon says she can thrive in. "It's a very welcoming place," she says. "It's my favorite city in Ireland."

Wide Open

Ray Giffen has fire in his belly about the power of the arts and the empowerment of communities, too. He wants Belfasters to gain the confidence to go to the nice theaters in the nice parts of town. He says he wants them to know, "It's yours — it's your taxes. I paid for it, you paid for it. Bring your kids here and get a bit of knowledge. They will grow up and they

will learn all they need to know about culture."

A fan of traditional music for at least 15 years, Giffen is equally as sharp about any perceived sectarian divide in regard to accessing the music. "The wide-held belief that traditional music belongs to one side? No it doesn't." He grins and sips coffee. "It belongs where people are suffering, where people need to rise up and speak out. That's what folk music is, that's why I love it."

Stan MacBroom, who runs music sessions at the Skainos Centre, echoes that sentiment. "Music has always been a part of Ireland's culture," he says. "[And] storytelling has also formed a big part [of

Uillean pipers jam at the Sunflower.

our culture], and singing, and poetry. A good session to me would have a good combination of all of those art forms."

At a recent Skainos session, MacBroom introduced himself, as the fiddles and whistles and bodhráns were being unpacked, and pointed me in the direction of the friendly gaggle at the tea and biscuits. True to his word, the night was full of music, storytelling, and poetry, and plenty of support for whoever was playing. I left around 11 p.m. to head to the Sunflower, and the Skainos party was still in full flow. I later learned it continued another two hours.

As I walked through Belfast to reach the Sunflower, I tried remembering how

different it was back during the Troubles — how limited and colorless and stark. But I couldn't remember. So much has changed. Case in point: I walked past a gay bar when a couple of people spilled out onto the road and handed me a badge that said "Love Equality NI" — supporting the campaign for marriage equality — and my mind moved on to other things. But I know, in the end, it's all about trying to be in the moment, sustained by our traditions and our shared culture, our shared music.

I like to think that my friend from the Horslips concert has his windows wide open these days, and he's listening to whatever he likes. ∎

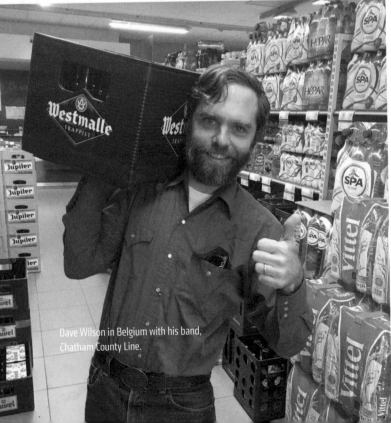

Dave Wilson in Belgium with his band,
Chatham County Line.

Home Away from Home

by Dave Wilson

n the slowly aging backstage of the Grote Post in Ostende, Belgium, an elderly woman leaned over me and asked, "Would you like some soup?"

I had been lying prostrate on a sofa, and cracked open a bleary eye. She was one of two ladies, clearly volunteers, tasked with caring for four road-weary North Carolina musicians who were thousands of miles from home.

"Why, sure," I replied, carefully rising to that slouched sitting position musicians on the road know so well. Her kindness and politeness was, I'd come to find, characteristic of Belgian audiences. After a little while, I knew if I asked her for a beer or two she would oblige.

It was Super Bowl Sunday and we had a matinee show to play. The crowd was hearty, and most of their hats held court over woolly patches of gray.

Onstage in a foreign country, I often wonder how much of the lyrics and banter an audience can truly understand, but they occasionally laugh and applaud — if not during a song, then excitedly after. I found this lack of responsiveness from the crowd confusing on my first trip overseas as a performer. After all, my band, Chatham County Line, comes from North Carolina, where, when that exciting moment surges within a song, someone is sure to yell or whistle. You'll get none of that in Belgium, where politeness is the unspoken rule. Instead, you focus a little harder on the craft and revel in the painstakingly designed and well-fortified acoustics of the music halls.

After the show, however, the crowd mobbed the merch table, and any fear I had that the audience did not understand us melted away in the face of their giddy desire for signed copies of our latest album and their embarrassed requests for photographs.

A knowing local in a Chuck Prophet T-shirt asked if I'd heard of his favorite local band. "They are Belgium's best bluegrass band," he added. I wrote their name on a piece of paper to be searched at some point when the Wi-Fi is free, and smiled to myself, because even this far from Bill Monroe's birthplace of Rosine, Kentucky, some local boys are still hammering out the hits.

After the show, we carried our instruments on a short walk to the hotel and agreed on a time to meet in the lobby. Unlike tours in the States, when a few rare extra hours of daytime can allow a visit to Willie's American Guitars in St. Paul or Picker's Supply in Fredericksburg, the one- and two-hour drives from town to town in Belgium leave too much time for the restless pursuits of the road.

In this case, because we played a matinee, we had a night to enjoy rather than scant daylight hours, so we headed off to the kafé in hopes of watching the Super Bowl. Granted, we're not major football fans. We're musicians who spend downtime ferreting out buried internet videos of the great banjoist Don Reno or guitarist Clarence White. Football is more of a distraction than a pursuit, but after two weeks overseas, everyone wouldn't mind a little slice of Americana.

The beer I landed on was called Jupiler, pronounced "who-pi-ler," but when the bartender heard our accents, he told us to say Jupiler and everyone got along. It's a pilsner, both clean and refreshing, and the only reason to order it in Belgium is when you've reached your limit of Trappist dubbels and tripels, each served in a freshly washed and branded chalice.

For beer drinkers, Belgium is heaven. You know that section of the bottle shop where every single beer costs as much as a domestic six-pack? That's what the menu at the Belgian kafé looks like, except the price is local.

Flush with euros from the night's merch sales, everyone started the evening at the long list of beers neatly scribed on a chalkboard and tried to outdo the others in authenticity and obscurity. Despite the initial reason we headed to the kafé, not one of us noticed there was no television for watching the game.

After a while, teeming with sudsy gold, we burst through the curtain and out into the street. John Teer, our mandolinist and last remaining bachelor, failed to meet any girls, so we decided to soothe his heartache with Belgian frites and shawarma.

And so it was a proper, standard ending to another night on tour in Belgium: Four American boys dripping mayonnaise and tzatziki on the cobblestones, laughing at some forgotten moment while walking past a casino window. Inside we could see a television, the Super Bowl blaring loudly in an empty room. ∎

THINGS WILL BE BETTER

David Broza's remarkable Mideast musical summit

by Lee Zimmerman

"We were raised to believe that the Palestinians hated us and wanted to wipe Israel off the face of the earth, and the Palestinians were taught to hate Jews and kill them and take over their land. So each side had its feelings about the others. Already we had a handicap. It was very difficult to look in one another's eyes and say, 'Hello there, let's have a coffee.' "
David Broza

Israeli singer-songwriter David Broza is a busy man with connections all over the world. He's performed with American roots music staples like Jackson Browne, Paul Simon, and Shawn Colvin. He was once flown back to Israel to split a bill with Bob Dylan so he could help sell out the venue. But in addition to his work alongside Americans, Broza has found meaningful success working with little-known artists on both the Israeli and Palestinian sides of Jerusalem.

Born in Israel, Broza grew up in England and Spain. His father was a businessman and his mother, Sharona Aaron, was a path-forging Israeli folksinger who introduced her young son to American artists like Odetta and Pete Seeger. Broza's grandfather co-founded the Neve Shalom/Wahat as-Salam Arab-Israeli peace settlement and helped start a regional youth movement. Spurred from his family's influence, the pursuits of business, peace, collaboration, and folk music have combined throughout the four decades of Broza's unique musical

career to make him one of Israel's most beloved singer-songwriters.

His career began in 1977, with his song, "Yihye Tov" ("Things Will Be Better"). Broza wrote the music to lyrics by Jonathan Geffen after Egyptian president Anwar Sadat broke ground with a peacemaking trip to Israel that year. The song established Broza as an important part of Israel's peace movement, increasing his notoriety as a musician, activist, and spokesperson for those who sought to build bridges with their Arab neighbors.

In the decades since, Broza has accelerated his musical reach, recording in Spanish as well as Hebrew and making inroads in the United States with several English-language albums — among them a collection of songs based on Townes Van Zandt's poetry. Broza and Van Zandt met in the mid-1990s, when folksinger and composer David Amram invited Broza to participate in a songwriters-in-the-round performance in Texas. Van Zandt was so impressed with Broza that he made a provision in his will that his poetry would be given to Broza to work with however he wished.

Broza released the resulting album, *Night Dawn: The Unpublished Poetry of Townes Van Zandt*, in 2010. But it was his most recent release, 2014's Steve Earle-produced *East Jerusalem/West Jerusalem* — which was accompanied by a documentary film about the making of the album — that was at the front of my mind when I spoke with him for this article. After all, in that nation divided by social, political, and religious ideology, the album accomplished more in an eight-day recording session than politicians have claimed in a half-century. The roots of the Israeli/Palestinian conflict run deep, and as Broza attests, many of the artists involved grew up believing folks on the opposite side of Jerusalem were their enemy. But for this project, Broza brought them together to create an album full of gripping, engaging music and a spirit of peace.

That's where our conversation began. It has been edited for clarity.

LEE ZIMMERMAN: What inspired you to create *East Jerusalem/West Jerusalem* — this collaboration between Israeli and Palestinian artists — and overcome the obvious animosities around politics and distrust?

DAVID BROZA: My engineer had been working with a group called Sabreen, the biggest Palestinian group in the world. [He] told me I had to meet the leader of the group and all his musicians. He said, "You guys are going to love each other." He didn't have any illusions about us working together, but he thought it would just be good for us to meet.

We met in the old city of Jerusalem and we hit it off in ... no time at all. [The leader of Sabreen, Said Murad,] invited me to come to his studio, and that started a relationship that's been going on 17 years. Over the course of the 17 years, we didn't play that much music together, but it inspired me to move my

projects to East Jerusalem because I felt so comfortable in that studio. I started to work there and hang out there, drink lots of wine and lots of coffee, had lots of barbecues and then I got this idea. I literally forced my Israeli musicians, who would never join this group on that side of the world. I had to twist their arms to come with me to spend eight days and eight nights in the studio. I said, "Listen guys, this is going to be good."

We had a psychological barrier, and it's something that's very human. We were raised to believe that the Palestinians hated us and wanted to wipe Israel off the face of the earth, and the Palestinians were taught to hate Jews and kill them and take over their land. So each side had its feelings about the others. Already we had a handicap. It was very difficult to look in one another's eyes and say, "Hello there, let's have a coffee."

We needed to go through a process and tear down those walls, those barriers. It was easier to get to the moon!

But I convinced them to go, and every time they had another condition like, "Oh, our wives won't let us go," I said "Bring your wives." And when they said, "The wives won't let us unless we bring the babies." I said, "Bring the babies. Bring the mother-in-law. Bring whoever."

I rented three-quarters of the hotel for the families and they were all there. There were 40 of us, and the band consisted of only four musicians! It was one of those things where I said I don't care what it takes. I've got Steve Earle, I've got the songs, and I'm sure the musicians will come once we're all set up and ready to go.

The first few days it was awkward, but they eventually found out that the people were really, really nice. Everybody was cool. We had Israeli cameramen, we had Palestinian cameramen, we had soundmen, and that was it. It was beautiful. Over time, those fears just melted away.

LZ: The break-in period must still have been awkward at first, no?

DB: We would limit ourselves to recording two or three songs a day so everyone could get acquainted.

We all got a chance to introduce ourselves and get to know one another. "Lets have a glass of wine, let's share a joke." And that's what happened. So the next day we would come into the studio and we would recognize the person we were sitting with the day before, and started to talk again. It was so easy to heal.

LZ: Did politics ever enter the mix?

DB: We started recording on Jan. 20, 2015, and on the 22nd, Israel started elections. We had to break down the studio and everyone went back home to where they could vote. We came back that night, and even though we hadn't recorded anything, dinner was waiting for us.

Frankly, we [didn't] allow any of it [into the room]. When you're working with people who have a certain sensitivity, you don't raise those issues. It was a form of psychotherapy.

LZ: Because those troubling tensions are almost omnipresent, I imagined the political tension might have been a daily occurrence. Like maybe some kind of comment would slip out ...

DB: No. We were all on guard and we were all wary. We've all been exposed to those harsh situations, so we're all aware. Plus, we're all artists. None of us are politicians. I'm not into politics. I'm into social issues, and, honestly, that's all that interests me.

Some of us want to make a living doing whatever, but the rest of us just want to make a living as an artist. I don't have any interest in having a discussion that I know will lead nowhere because I'm not a politician. I have discussions about social issues. Why is the garbage not being picked up? Why aren't the schools good enough? I have those discussions, because [those things] are under Israeli control.

This is about us. It's about getting health services and social services and getting a good education. We share the same issues. Whether we're Palestinian or whether we're Jews, we're living under the same flag and we're paying taxes and we ought to be getting those services. So we fight that fight together.

LZ: Did you get any pushback from the people back home, about working with Palestinians and vice versa?

DB: There was hesitance, especially from some other musicians. But Palestinians told us that the studio was ours, and I believe, as the proverbs say, that time is always of the essence. Don't pay attention to a week, a month, or a year. Let's just take the journey.

Now that the film [about the making of the album] is out, there's no telling who sees what. Everything is more relaxed, people have come to realize that when you do it from the heart and there are no organizations involved, the people can reach out to other people. [That's] a lot easier to explain. There's a lot less negativity and we see we can do more projects. And I hope we will do more.

LZ: It seems that now that you've done it once, you could make it part of your regular recording regimen.

DB: It is. I've been going to that studio for over 17 years and I haven't stopped. I'll be there next week and I'll be working with kids in [Palestinian]

refugee camps, and my buddies, and [we'll] continue the conversation and continue the love, and continue the compadre attitude.

We're in this together and we're making music. Now our children can see this is a normal thing and can take [it to] the next level.

LZ: Considering the political animosity between Israel and Palestine, is it scary for an Israeli to go to the Palestinian camps in East Jerusalem?

DB: Generally speaking, it's not. I continue to go to the refugee camp, but some of those tend to be very violent and very disturbing, so they're not safe for anybody. We bring the children to the studio, where we can work with them safely and quietly, and not have to worry about anyone who's disturbed, [who] might pick up a knife or a rifle. We stay out of harm's way as much as we can.

LZ: Is there any kind of security?

DB: No, because security won't help. Violence can happen anywhere — [just like] in East L.A., for example. These are densely populated areas where there are a lot of people who are angry, and they don't have a chance to express themselves, so they walk out and do horrible things. But we're not part of military operations or police operations. I have a guitar on my back. I've come there to play. I'm there to soothe the mind and massage the heart, and open up people's eyes.

LZ: In the US, we see the headlines and the animosity, so it's good to get another perspective. The fact that you're able to break down barriers — it's very special and unique.

DB: Some of the things that we've learned from living here are the kind of things you can only learn in these conditions, no matter whether you're a musician or an educator or what have you.

If I was asked to areas likeBogotá or Medellín or troubled neighborhoods in the US, I would go without thinking twice and I'd bring everything I know. If

we can do it in Israel, we can do it with Latinos, with African-Americans, with poor and underprivileged people, wherever they are.

We can all live on knowledge, because there's a lot of knowledge to go around.

LZ: Not many artists can maintain their success for decades, as you have. It's hard to stay relevant and in the public eye. What's allowed you to keep that momentum?

DB: First of all, I'm an artist, and I will be for the rest of my life. I have a vision and I have to accomplish it, and [that] can take years, but I keep working at it until I succeed.

After my first big hit, when I had two kids and I was 26 or 27, I realized I could have hits and live a good life, but there was something missing in my private world, which was knowledge. The only way that I could get that knowledge was to explore the music and get to the source. That was American folk, American jazz, and then there was Jimi Hendrix and Charlie Parker and Cannonball Adderley, and eventually Joni Mitchell and The Band and the Beatles. So I went through all these different phases and I was being exposed and influenced.

When I was 22 and writing my own music, I had to lean on the harmonies that I had learned from folk people like James Taylor and Paul Simon. Then I wanted to find out where it all came from. That's when I started coming here to the States, around '84, and so I brought my Israeli music, which was already influenced by American folk and jazz and all that, and tried to connect with the American listener. But [that's] a lot harder than you think. I had to go to the Midwest, I had to go to the Deep South, I had to go to Texas, and sometimes it was horrible. I'd play these little tiny holes in the wall. I came from playing to 3,000 people a night [in Israel], yet I had to remove myself from that world to understand what I was

"I don't think [music] can change the world, but if you ask me if there can be peace in the world, then I'd say come with me to East Jerusalem and you'll feel only peace. That's the world I live in. It's not about changing the planet, but more about changing people's ways of thinking."

here for. It was [like] school.

I learned American poetry because I didn't trust my own voice. I'd go to whatever bookstore I could find and go straight to the poetry section. I'd discover a new poet every day and then I'd start writing music to these things. I'd connect with wherever these poets came from. One was from Denver. One was from Baltimore. One was from Seattle.

Before I knew it, 17 years went by and I was recording American poetry on my albums. Then I'd go back to Tel Aviv each month for 10 days of shows. I'd keep in touch with my audience so they wouldn't think I had disappeared.

LZ: What prompted you to start recording in Spanish?

DB: When I was 12, my family moved to Spain. That's where I spent my formative years. My Spanish wasn't that great, because I went to an English school. Then I went into the army, I became an artist, I got married, I had kids. There was a 25-year gap from the time I left Spain, but I really wanted to start writing in Spanish and reconnect with the country.

I went back there, and I met a singer-songwriter, Jorge Drexler, in Spain and he became a friend of mine. He was actually a Hawaiian musician who moved to Spain. He was Jewish and he heard me sing on a radio show, and he got in touch with me. I asked him if he would like to write with me.

The album on which [our] song appeared [*Spanish Heart*] was a very big success and it became a big hit in Spain. So suddenly I was a Spanish artist and I then had to master the language. I went from town to town to perform — all

these very small towns where they only spoke Spanish. I became more familiar with the language and the culture, and I ended up making three albums there.

LZ: You've recorded with the Andalusian Orchestra, you recorded the poetry of Townes Van Zandt, you do albums in Spanish, English, and Hebrew. How do you constantly switch gears?

DB: When I moved to the States, I began researching the poets. I fell in love with the culture of the heartland and the depth of this country and the vastness and the heavy-duty culture. It's not just what's in the books, it's the day-to-day language, the way people talk to you, the way the culture moves from Corpus Christi to Michigan. There's a diversity, but in a very subtle way, because it's all one land. There are mountains, deserts, plains. People in the Ozarks speak a different language than the people out west, and I find it fascinating. I immersed myself in that.

LZ: But then you had a terrible accident that waylaid your career.

DB: I went back to Israel and I was in a horrible car crash, and that put me out of commission for quite a while. I lost all my contacts in [the US]. I wasn't able to play. My lungs collapsed. I was practically paralyzed. I was in a bad state. But I chose to look on the bright side. It gave me a chance to chill out, and slowly I got better. I got back to playing.

But that explains why I suddenly wrapped up here and went back to Spain. I sold my house in New Jersey and moved back to Spain. And then I had to get reacquainted with Spain, so I really immersed myself in Spanish art, music, and poetry. I got to know the best

Spanish musicians. They all helped me with my poetry and songwriting, [which is] difficult to decipher. It's got the culture, it's got the country, it's got the blues. ... I mean, what is that? It was very confusing.

The record companies have a hard time with me because I don't follow the formula. When I had my biggest-selling album, they expected me to have another one like that. But I was too young to be interested in that. I was ready to move on to the next thing. These days I will do sequel after sequel after sequel, but when I was young, I'd just do albums that would interest me for the sheer integrity and the ability to bring my music to as many people as possible, to make my guitar playing as good as possible.

My next album is going to be all instrumental. There's not going to be any singing. And then I'll do my next Spanish album, my next Hebrew album, my next American album. I'll just keep on going.

My new single was recorded in July 1998, "A Long Road," with Maura O'Connell. We were going to record an entire album together, but then that August, I had that terrible accident. So nothing gets lost. Now it's going to be out. Nothing is wasted, even when it's from 18 years ago.

LZ: It's fascinating how you made that journey.

DB: This is how I immerse myself in three cultures. I'll hang out with American poets over here, and I'll be on the front lines with Israeli and Palestinian musicians over there. This is it. I live these different experiences and bring them out in the form of songs and

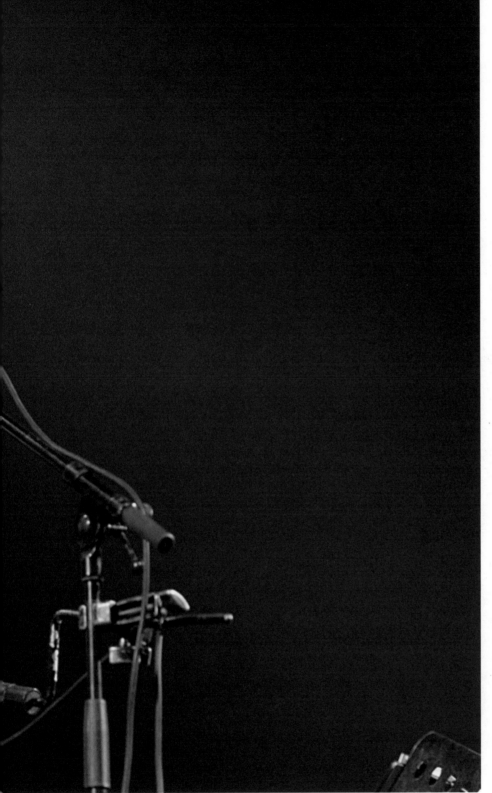

performance.

LZ: You really believe in the power of music. A lot of people talk the talk but you obviously believe it.

DB: I don't think [music] can change the world, but if you ask me if there can be peace in the world, then I'd say come with me to East Jerusalem and you'll feel only peace. That's the world I live in.

It's not about changing the planet, but more about changing people's ways of thinking. One at a time, or a hundred at a time. But you have to see them, you have to touch them, you have to be a part of them, and it takes time — it may take me a lifetime. So what? It's worth every minute, every breath I take. It's the journey I'm doing.

I have many friends who talk about the experiences they've read about, but I suggest, "Why don't you just go live it and see how you come out of it?" You can't take other people's misery and take it on as your own.

Steve Earle almost died by following in what he thought was Townes Van Zandt's footsteps, but he was lucky, because he was arrested and put in jail. Unfortunately, Townes didn't get locked up to amend his terrible, self-destructive fate.

I realized about 10 years ago that I mastered my craft, and now it's time to master my art. This is the way I live. It's the ABC of my everyday life and it doesn't take me away from my kids, my family, my love for my wife and friends, but it's always in my head. People know they can always find me with my guitar at any given moment. ∎

A BEAUTIFUL SUIT

Amira Medunjanin makes traditional music to fit modern Bosnia

by Megan Romer

AMIRA MEDUNJANIN IS ON the vanguard of the revival of sevdah music, an ancient folk ballad tradition born in the fecund cultural crossroads of Bosnia and Herzegovina. Though unschooled, Medunjanin sings with a clarity and control most trained vocalists strive for across a lifetime. The songs to which she's dedicated her life are powerful, lyrical tales of love and loss.

The word "sevdah" comes from the same Arabic root ("al sawda," meaning black and referring to black bile, the ancient source of melancholy) as the Portuguese word "saudade" (wistful nostalgia, longing), which is the constant theme of the similarly expressive fado music. Both of these disparate genres bear more lyrical similarities to early jazz and blues, and even the laments of country and western music, than they do the historical ballads that are more commonly associated with traditional Western folk music. And while sevdah music is not yet widely known in the States, its themes are certainly universal.

"It doesn't matter if the songs were actually born in Bosnia and Herzegovina, for example, or any other country of ex-Yugoslavia," Medunjanin says. "The messages in there are so universal, and can be applied in Uganda, can be applied in Argentina, or USA, anywhere. It's just the normal basic values of life — good life — and being a good person."

Indeed, Medunjanin's fiery interpretations of this traditional form have enchanted audiences around Europe, and as of late 2016, in the United States and Canada as well. Her latest album, *Damar,* is available on World Village Records.

Recently we spoke over the phone about how she came to this music and what has inspired her to keep spreading it throughout the world, how the unrest in her native country has moved her music, and so much more.

The interview has been edited for

length and clarity.

MEGAN ROMER: During the Siege of Sarajevo, you were a teenager? I know you were young.

AMIRA MEDUNJANIN: I was in my 20s. I was 19½ when it started.

MR: I was reading about how in that time, there was a huge underground music scene in Sarajevo, but, like, literally underground, right?

AM: Well, yes, that was the only way to do it! But you felt a bit like Hobbits. [laughs] ... It wasn't every night. It was when we could get out of the houses and go to a certain place where we'd gather up. But there were many concerts held. And you know, there was no electricity, so sometimes we would use car batteries, and then charge them up with a bicycle.

MR: Wait, you'd take turns riding?

AM: Yeah! But it was such a great time. I have to be honest, I never talk about the war time. I really try to put it behind me. I always try to remember the nice things, only the nice things. I remember how much fun we had, and how much laughter we had while doing that! You know, [asking] who's going to be next, and then pulling out straws for who's going to do the bicycle thing to create some light.

But it was fantastic! We would gather up — sometimes just guitars, acoustic guitars — and sit there, even not in a basement, sometimes just sit on the stairs of an apartment building, depending on which area we were gathering.

[Then] there were some, like, Rock Under Siege scenes and there were some fantastic concerts held. When you'd find someone a little more resourceful, they'd find ways to put the amplifiers and stuff [on stage], so there were concerts happening. And I would attend all of them. That was like a celebration for us, any time we'd have a chance.

MR: Can you talk to me a little bit about sevdah?

AM: It's a musical tradition — an oral tradition that has been, according to the records that we have, existing in Bosnia and Herzegovina for five centuries. It's influenced by different cultures that were living in that area throughout that time. You can feel the meeting of the Orient and Occident world — the Eastern and Western world are meeting there. We're very lucky to have that location, that geographical position. Well, and [also] unlucky, you know. [Laughs.]

Throughout the history, when you look back, ... it was invaded quite a lot. First it was the Ottoman Empire, then Austro-Hungarian Empire. ... But I always try to see good things in bad things. The good thing is that the musical culture was enriched enormously. You have, as I said before, Oriental influence in there, lots of Gypsy influence in there — it's really a melting pot of different cultures. We were very lucky with that, because we got this beautiful music.

You can also find the traces of Sephardic music. The Sephardim fled Spain five centuries ago and they settled down in Bosnia, and they brought their own tradition. It's just unbelievably beautiful.

You have to have that history in order to make that kind of music. ... The songs were always passed down from generation to generation. My mother taught me the majority of the songs. Her mother taught her. There are some written traces of the lyrics, but it's very hard to find the exact time when the exact songs actually came about. Most of them are written by unknown authors. Most of them have been changing, evolving over the centuries, adding different versions of the text and lines by the folk, by the people. So the versions that we have today are probably the really, really, really extended versions of the original ones.

But they never lose the essence of the beautiful poetry — and it's really beautiful poetry. It's a tradition that, back in those days, was reserved for the urban wealthy people. The singers would come to their houses, for whatever occasion. Women were not singers; at that time only men were allowed to sing. Later on, women came on the scene too. It was originally just a cappella versions, [then] came the instrument called saz, which is a stringed instrument like a lute, very similar to a lute, [from] the Ottoman Empire. Later on, with the Austro-Hungarians, the accordion came. So it really evolved over time. But that essence — the authentic melody, the authentic lyrics, the form, the body — remained intact.

MR: I feel like a lot of people who don't know about folk music traditions around the world think of folk music as a museum thing, or a preservation piece. Something that only tells a story of a thing that happened, that has no relevance today, and is only important because it helps us remember something. But, listening to sevdah — and other forms too, like Portuguese fado and flamenco and Ladino, and blues and jazz — even if the stories are old, they have a certain universality. A story can be old but also explain something that has relevance today.

AM: Exactly. I couldn't agree more. The messages are so universal, even now.

When I was 5 years old, 30-something years ago, even though the song was written down 400 years ago, I [could] find things that matter to me. The messages are so universal.

I am totally against ... when they say traditional music of one country or folk music of one country should be kept in a beautiful golden chest and you pull it out only when there is some national celebration, just to remember it. ... That's what happened in my country, you know? And I am so annoyed with it, because I really consider it a living form. It's a live thing. It should be allowed to evolve and it should be allowed to breathe today, and to develop.

How do we know how these songs sounded five centuries ago? We don't! We don't have the records. We don't know how they actually came about — the really, really, really original versions. So I am totally against [the idea] that they should be preserved and kept in a golden chest.

MR: It's not the good silverware!

AM: Absolutely not, no.

I wouldn't say I'm the black sheep, but some purists and traditionalists wouldn't agree with me, and they would often attack me, in a way, [saying,] "This is not proper sevdah, what did you do with it? Why do you use piano?" Because why not? Why not? I could use silence as well ...

MR: I joke sometimes about purism in folk music, about how if musicians one hundred years ago or five hundred years ago had the technology we have today, they would have used it. They absolutely would have. They would have wanted to, because it sounded good! Because it's fun! Because why not?

This idea of purist folk culture is a very new one. And I don't think many purists understand how ironic this is. People were always excited to have new music and new instruments — when the accordion was invented, it went everywhere. Everyone liked it! It was loud, it filled a room, what's not to like?

AM: You should hear the story about my accordion session. My accordion episodes in life.

MR: Oh, do you play accordion?

AM: No, I don't play accordion. I never liked accordion as an instrument, how it was played in these songs. It was overplayed. It was covering everything up

> **"Traditional sevdah is such a beautiful, fruitful soil for interpretation. It's a very free form for the vocalist. You can use your own expressions. … A certain song, when you read the lyrics, the film that you see in your head leads you to this instrumental part around it. Like you're creating a beautiful suit for a certain body."**
>
> Amira Medunjanin

with too many ornaments. [It was] too loud, too aggressive. I really never liked it, so I never had it in the group. Until once, I found a girl who was playing classical contemporary accordion. And I was like, "Mmmm, that sounds good!" I recorded an album, just classical contemporary accordion and vocals — sevdah music. Boy, everybody hated me for it.

MR: Of course they did! You monster!

AM: [Laughing.] "You monster! What did you do?! This is not accordion! What is this? This is not a proper accordion!" I said, "Yes, it is accordion!" "No, it's not!" "Yes, it is! Look, I've got the pictures! I've got some video!"

MR: It's funny to me that anyone would be a purist about the accordion. I mean it's what, only 130, 160 years old? It's not even an ancient instrument. By folk standards, it's a very young instrument.

AM: But it's absolutely gorgeous. I love this contemporary classical accordion, it's just gorgeous.

MR: Your way of playing sevdah in particular is very contemporary-sounding to me. You use jazz influence, different kinds of things from around the world. Where do you find the things you are adding?

AM: The music I listen to apart from sevdah, the music I like, the musicians I'm

fortunate enough to work with, they have wonderful ideas. I'm not a fan of sorting music in genres, putting it on shelves, adding labels. I love good music, the music that moves me. If my heart goes trembling, that's good music for me, regardless if it's coming from the classical world, or the jazz world, or the rock world, or even pop. … If the song is good, it moves me, I listen to it.

As I said earlier with this traditional music, I think it's such a beautiful living form that can be shown in different lights. Traditional sevdah is such a beautiful, fruitful soil for interpretation. It's a very free form for the vocalist. You can use your own expressions. … A certain song, when you read the lyrics, the film that you see in your head leads you to this instrumental part around it. Like you're creating a beautiful suit for a certain body, yeah?

For me, it's like that. I simply hear things. One of the songs that we created, with a piano player I've worked with for eight years, Bojan Zulfikarpašic [known as Bojan Z]. He's a jazz pianist, and he's very free in his playing and composing, and he adds elements from folk music from around here. But he adds it so beautifully, so subtly … it's not cheesy, you know what I mean? It's not trying to please anyone, it's trying to please this beautiful

suit around this song, around this body.

MR: So it's very organic for you, right? You're not saying, "Oh, I must add jazz to this song."

AM: Oh, no, it's very, very, very, extremely organic for me. … Bojan and I, we met one day before our first concert together. I met him, let's say, tonight at 8 o'clock, I meet him, and tomorrow at 8 o'clock we are performing in a sold-out concert hall, you see? So I ask him over to dinner, and I said, "What are we going to play tomorrow?" And he said, "Just give me the list of the songs that you would like to play. I might know all of them, but I might not!" [Laughs.]

These were all traditional pieces, and he's also originating from this part of the world. He was born in Belgrade, but over 30 years now he has lived in France. … He says, "Do you trust me?" I said, "Yes. Sure."

So we went on stage next day, and, really, it was one of the best concerts we ever had. It was just him and me and piano and silence, and it was just crazy.

This energy happened. We created something very beautiful. Without planning … to add this element to the music or that, I start to sing and he starts to go, and we were really — how do you say? Complementing. I need a better word.

MR: Confluence? Synchronicity?

AM: Yeah! Exactly! I would start the phrase with singing, and ... without knowing the phrase, he would finish it in his own way, and it was exactly the same tune I had in my head. Which is, like, really scary.

MR: It seems so rare to be able to find musical soulmates like that; people who can complete your musical thoughts. ... It's sort of like when you fall in love and suddenly realize that another person can see inside your head a little bit? Like, "I've been alone here inside my brain all these years, and now here you are."

AM: And ... you know the feeling, like your heart starts beating, crazy beating, and that someone calls you? That's spooky to me. I'm 44 and I'm still spooked like that. [Laughs.]

MR: You just visited North America for the first time in late fall and just got back from your second trip. You were here for the election, right? It must have been so strange to watch basically the entire country lose our minds.

AM: Yeah, I was there on the 8th [of November], the final election day. I saw the people doing demonstrations, but I had that for many, many years in my country so for me, this is just like a normal day. This is a normal thing!

MR: But it must be so strange for you coming from someplace where much of your life was during wartime, or at least living under corrupt government, so watching us lose our minds over this election, from both political directions, even ...

AM: You know what, I am an irreparable optimist in life, and that's something that I learned in those four years that I had [during the Siege]. It was quite an expensive school, but it was a good school for me. The good always has to prevail. There will be crazy times, and crazy times are everywhere at any point. [Bosnians] overcame our issues, I think. We have normal peaceful time and live together. So anything is possible, if the people come to their senses and they stand up together.

There's some talk in my country now, crazy talk, but I think people are just tired of going into the troubles again, and I want to believe that. We're just here for a very, very, very short time, so ... [that's] really just wasting time. It's good to waste time to enjoy yourself — that time is not actually wasted. But I think there's still really a lot of light in this world. I'm an irreparable optimist. I do believe in love! I really do! [Laughs.] What can I do? I'm just a hopeless romantic! ■

REBUILDING MUSIC

**Afghan youth orchestra
finds peace amid violence
and revives hope for the future**

by Hilary Saunders

PHOTOS BY LE MARIN PRODUCTIONS - MARIN RAGUZ

THE DAY BEFORE DR. AHMAD Naser Sarmast had scheduled a Skype interview for this article, two suicide bombers blew themselves up in Kabul. The first attack took place near a police station in the southwestern part of Afghanistan's capital, while the second blast shook the eastern side of the city, near the National Directorate of Security. Afghan officials told *The New York Times* that 23 people were killed and 106 were wounded.

Sarmast, the founder and director of the Afghanistan National Institute of Music (ANIM) is, unfortunately, all too familiar with such attacks. He survived a suicide-bombing attempt during a performance at the Centre d'Enseignement Français en Afghanistan, a Franco-Afghan school in Kabul, back in 2014. The pianist, trumpeter, teacher, and music administrator nearly lost his hearing in the blast, and underwent emergency surgery to correct much of the damage.

The bombings didn't really affect daily routines within ANIM. We had to find another time for our interview, but that was mainly because Sarmast had a busy day, and the nine-and-a-half-hour time difference between Kabul and New York City didn't help.

When we managed to connect via a WhatsApp-powered audio call a few days later, Sarmast stated, rather objectively: "Well, we're working in a war zone, and it happens from time to time. We are continuing to work.

"Day to day, we're not even thinking about what's going on around us," he adds. "There's not a suicide bomber every day. It happens from time to time, but generally the situation is not bad."

Still, this is the reality that ANIM faces as it tries to teach music to Afghan youth and provide them with safe spaces to learn and perform. Since April 2008, the institute has been functioning as an organization within the Afghanistan Department of Education, with additional support from the Deputy Ministry for Technical Vocation and Educational Training. But providing music education for Afghan youth has been Sarmast's passion for much longer than these nine years.

As the son of one of Afghanistan's most recognized conductors, songwriters, and composers, Ustad Salim Sarmast, the younger Sarmast grew up surrounded by music. He graduated from music school in Afghanistan, earned a master's degree in musicology from Moscow State Conservatory, and eventually was granted asylum in Australia before earning his doctorate in music from Monash University in Melbourne — according to him, the first Afghan ever to earn a Ph.D. in music.

With asylum papers, Sarmast could have stayed in Australia. But having fled his home in the midst of the Afghan civil war — which ravaged the country from 1996 to 2001, as the Taliban captured Kabul — Sarmast knew he had to come back if he truly wanted the culture to change.

"When I returned to Afghanistan from Australia back in 2008," he says, "from the very beginning I was very eager to provide music education to boys and girls of Afghanistan regardless of their gender, social circumstances, or religious sects."

As it stands now, ANIM is one of the largest, safest, most important music education facilities in the country. Sarmast likes to call it "the happiest place in Afghanistan," even in the same breath as noting that he and ANIM are both on the Taliban's hit list. These days, 250 students — about a third of whom are young women — study at ANIM and perform in eight ensembles. The faculty

Zarifa Adiba (center) directs Ensemble Zohra.

consists of 40 locals and expats who teach Western music, Afghan music, and general education, as well as 15 other support staff members.

In addition to support from national organizations, ANIM boasts a diverse roster of international backers. The World Bank is the largest funding body, but Germany's Goethe Institute, the British Consul, the embassies of Finland and Demark, and the Indian Council for Cultural Relations have all collaborated with ANIM and/or offered financial assistance. To boot, the US Embassy in

Kabul is ANIM's second-biggest economic backer, awarding project-based grants to the organization since 2011, including English-language music instruction (seen as beneficial for encouraging young Afghans to explore and learn in Western musical environments), instrument repair clinics, and more.

"One element in our public diplomacy programming in Afghanistan is to help preserve the country's incredibly rich and historically important cultural heritage, ... both the tangible — such as monuments and archeological sites — and the

intangible, such as music," says Terry Davidson, a spokesman for US Embassy Kabul, via email.

Reviving Tradition

Historical, musical, and cultural preservation is at the heart of ANIM's multipurpose mission. Although the country enjoyed a rich musical heritage for centuries, culminating in the golden age of the 1970s-1980s, the Taliban outright banned music from 1996 to 2001. This included each of the three main types of music in Afghanistan: popular music that Sarmast compares to Bollywood pop, classical music that shares Hindustani theoretical and philosophical principles, and music of the people or regions of Afghanistan.

Although that dialectical music is most comparable to what Americans would describe as folk music, the traditions within Afghan classical music are important markers of "roots," as well. Sarmast explains that much of classical and regional Afghan music is passed orally from generation to generation. When the Taliban banned all music, the regime not only silenced Afghans at that time, but also stunted the passage of information and musical traditions.

The Taliban "deprived the people of Afghanistan of their very basic human rights — to listen to music, to practice music, and to learn music," explains Sarmast. "In other words, they silenced the people of Afghanistan and they prevented the people of Afghanistan from singing."

As a result of this political oppression (as well as technological advances and shifting cultural preferences), the future of Afghanistan's most authentic musical traditions remains threatened.

"The classical tradition is in danger of becoming obsolete in Afghanistan," says Sarmast. "That's why one of the objects of the Afghanistan Institute of Music is to impart the classical tradition of Afghanistan ... and make sure it is transmitted from the aging master musicians to the younger generation through a formal music education program."

The Afghan Youth Orchestra is the largest ensemble that ANIM supports. The first of its kind in more than 30 years, the group consists of both boys and girls playing a combination of traditional Afghan and Western classical instruments. The traditional instruments include stringed instruments like the robab, oud, and sitar, the harmonium-like dutat, and percussion such as zerbaghali and tabla. Using Western and traditional

Afghan instruments, they've performed works by Ravel, Vivaldi's *The Four Seasons,* and even Beethoven's "Ode to Joy" on their most recent tour to the World Economic Forum in Davos, Switzerland, and then on to Zurich, Geneva, Berlin, and Weimar.

But it's Ensemble Zohra, the all-girl youth orchestra named after the goddess of music in parts of Afghan and Persian culture, that stands in greatest defiance of musical suppression and gender inequality in Afghanistan. As the country's first all-female group, Ensemble Zohra is comprised of about 30 girls between 13 and 20 years old and performs Western and traditional Afghan music.

In a region where early marriages, domestic violence, sexual harassment, and other manifestations of gender bias proliferate, education is one of the most effective ways to combat such issues. Still, educational opportunities — especially in music — remain extremely unequal.

"In many parts of Afghanistan, girls are not allowed to have access to general education," Sarmast says. "We are living and working in a country where, in most of the provinces, girls are not allowed to continue their education after grade six. We are working in a country where music was banned and women were deprived from every human right. We are working in a country which is strongly segregated based on gender." His voice rises passionately. "But the Afghanistan Institute of Music is one, if I'm not overstating, among a few organizations that are supporting coed education and is strongly committed to empowering boys and girls through music."

Although boys can find private music education in Afghanistan, girls are still not allowed any educational resources. "For girls, there's not a safe environment within the community to study music, to be part of a musical ensemble, and to make a contribution to the musical environment of Afghanistan," explains Sarmast. "That's why we are very much committed to contribute to gender equality in

Afghanistan and to the empowerment of girls to music and education."

Peace through Music

Just as Sarmast seemed unafraid amid the most recent suicide bombings, Zohra conductor and violist Zarifa Adiba pronounces her fearlessness in performing in a place with such regular violence. The 18-year-old speaks in quick English with a confidence that's audible, even when she laments that her language skills need to improve before she applies to universities in the United States.

"I've given interviews to maybe hundreds of media and all of them have asked me this question!" she chides when I probe about the lingering influence of the Taliban's extremism. "At first I was really shocked about this because music is something in Afghanistan right now that is the only key that can bring peace inside you. You are hearing blasts, firings, news from the media. ... In these situations, the only thing that can give you peace is music.

"When I take my viola, when I am sitting with the girls in Zohra ensemble and we practice, that's the only time that we are feeling relaxed, without worrying about anything, and we just enjoy our lives," she adds. "But when you get out of ANIM, you can see street harassment. You can see everything completely differently than sitting in orchestra with Zohra. That's why I think that music is the only key that can bring peace inside me and everybody in ANIM, and also for the country."

Adiba grew up in Pakistan, but came to Ghazni, a city a few hours outside of Kabul, in 2012, before moving to the capital in 2014. A multi-instrumentalist, she first began playing the flute, but switched to viola about two and a half years ago. She began conducting less than a year ago.

Even as a child, Adiba loved music. "When I was in Pakistan," she says, "I used to sing in a chorus and I was very interested in arts. But I didn't know that that's what music is! I was living in Quetta, which is a city of Pakistan where a lot of

> **"Music is something in Afghanistan right now that is the only key that can bring peace inside you. You are hearing blasts, firings, news from the media. ... In these situations, the only thing that can give you peace is music."**
>
> Zarifa Adiba

Afghan people are living. ... In high school I was singing songs during the assembly and stuff like that, but usually I was singing songs at home — while cooking or cleaning the house.

"When I moved to Afghanistan," she continues, "I took the decision that I wanted to be a top singer. I was trying to find a vocal teacher in Kabul, but then I found out about ANIM and I was so excited that I was going to join a music school here! I never imagined that in Afghanistan they were going to have this school this soon."

Role Models

For Adiba and the other members of the Ensemble Zohra, just seeing other young women in music is vital to female empowerment and long-standing change in Afghanistan, Pakistan, and many regions throughout Central Asia. But that notion isn't geographically limited. Courtney Hartman — guitarist and vocalist in the all-women American bluegrass/folk group Della Mae — recalls that even growing up in Colorado, seeing a female presence in music helped her forge her own career.

Calling from Brooklyn before a brief run of solo shows opening for banjoist Noam Pikelny, Hartman says, "When I was 10 or 11, I saw a girl playing guitar, a woman playing guitar. And it's not that that's what made me play guitar, necessarily. But in my mind, I looked at her and I said, 'Oh! I can do that! I'll do that!' I don't understand how that works, but I think there's power in just seeing someone that you can relate to."

During Della Mae's participation in a US State Department-run American Music

Abroad (AMA) tour to Pakistan, Uzbekistan, Turkmenistan, Kazakhstan, Kyrgyzstan, and Tajikistan in 2012, Hartman remembered her initial reaction to seeing someone like herself playing music. Then, through the band's subsequent AMA tours to Saudi Arabia in 2014 and Brazil in 2016, and now, she uses those memories as motivation to share that inspiration.

"If I can do that personally, or if Della Mae can do that to young girls here in the States or [for] women in Saudi Arabia — whether that be musical or just them saying, 'Oh! I have a voice and I can use it!' in whatever way that is — that's why I think [women performing] is important."

It's working, too. By seeing, learning with, and performing alongside other young women in ANIM and Ensemble Zohra in particular, Adiba's dedication to gender equality has intensified. Now, she hopes to study psychology and music business in order to help change the culture in Afghanistan.

"When I started playing with Zohra orchestra, I just realized that there is no difference between boys and girls," Adiba says. "We all are human and we are born as a human. We all have human rights. And this is the biggest lesson that I've learned from Zohra, is to know yourself as a human, rather than being a girl or a daughter or sister or anything. So it's the most important thing that I'll never forget and forever I'll work for it in Afghanistan."

Still, it's the music itself that seems to speak loudest among the students at ANIM, its administrators and teachers, and those who discover the sounds of Afghanistan; theirs is the music of the people, after all.

"People ask us all the time, 'How could

you communicate musically with people from such different cultures or with such different languages?'" says Hartman. "And when you break down what folk music means, it's music and stories about folk, which is why the songs written a hundred years ago still translate to today. They're about struggle and triumph and love and sorrow. It's why our folk songs can feel very similar to the folk songs in Afghanistan or Kazakhstan or Vietnam."

The music wafting through the halls at ANIM represents the intersection of progressive education and historical and cultural preservation in Afghanistan. And as long as the music is not silenced there, it will continue to be transcribed, recorded, played, taught, and learned. It will help convey life skills of cross-cultural communication and collaboration. It will continue to help performers and listeners heal and find hope in unstable times.

"What brought me to Afghanistan is my strong belief in the 'soft power' of music," says Sarmast. "Almost every member of this nation, in one way or another, has been impacted by the war. [It's] a country that still lives under enormous stress, that at any moment anything might happen to our citizens. Therefore, I strongly belief in the healing power of music. I strongly believe that music and music education can help Afghans recover from the miseries of war and to forget about what they're experiencing every day ... and enormously contribute to their healing process.

"Music can teach our youths, our children, to respect each other and have respect for each other's differences," he adds, "[and] live in peace and harmony the same way they are playing in an orchestra." ∎

UmbriaJazz

Winter # 24

Orvieto

28 dicembre 2016 - 1° gennaio 2017

Deep inside Italy, a jazz festival plants new musical traditions

by Matt Powell

UMBRIA
IN BLUE

> **"The bishop and I sat down one night and drank an entire bottle of grappa. When we finished, the bishop agreed to the concerts, as long as he could give a Mass of peace."**
> Stefano Cimicchi

IT IS A COLD AND QUIET TUESDAY evening in that magical, nebulous week between Christmas and the New Year, when time and reality seem to hang in suspended animation. The city of Orvieto, Italy, shimmers with a celestial twinkle, small white lights strung across the high-walled streets like icicles, illuminating the dark cobblestones in a silver glow. Christmas trees stand majestic in the piazzas and "Christmas cribs" of all manner and size are erected in every crevice.

There is little indication that Italy's leading jazz festival — that any festival — is afoot.

Soon the sound of distant drums floats across the small city, joined by horns blowing a piper's call. The street band Funk Off begins its inaugural parade through town. Funk Off models itself on the New Orleans second line tradition, which itself has Italian roots. (The band name's off-color pun is lost in translation.)

The horn and drum riffs become louder as the band snakes through the winding streets. People fall in line,

growing in its wake until poured into the grand piazza.

The band faces the cathedral, or duomo, as if posing a challenge. Sinful rhythms of skin and brass reverberate off its facade. There is a casualness to the parade virtually impossible to encounter in contemporary America — no cones or barricades or police presence. It is a kind of jubilant, controlled chaos.

Umbria Jazz Winter is on.

Distant Drums

Umbria is a mystical, mountainous land of paradox. The only Italian region lacking a foreign or coastal border, the "green heart of Italy" is at once central and remote. Umbrian civilization dates back to the elusive Etruscans. What little we know of their advanced society is gleaned from their scant recovered art and science, like the intricate wells and underground caves of Orvieto.

The ancient Umbrians built their city-states on the tops of hills high above the green valleys, once flooded with lake water. As Romans and Barbarians sieged, the cities became fortified and insular. The original Umbrian city-states were perennially at war, with foreign invaders as well as with each other, creating an indigenous dichotomy: your nearest neighbor was your enemy. Much of this psychology remains in the inherent

COURTESY OF UMBRIA JAZZ

Teatro Mancinelli

competition among the hill cities comprising modern day Umbria: capital Perugia, sacred Assisi, majestic Gubbio. And Orvieto — *la città della rupe* ("the city of the cliff").

Umbria is a land of festivals, and each city has its own centuries-old celebrations. Music brings the region together. In the almost sacred month of May, the *Cantamaggio* ("Songs of May" festival) is still especially strong in

northern Umbria. Each April 30, musicians travel door-to-door, singing traditional folk songs. Umbrian folk music is rhythmic and mostly for dancing. The primary instrument a lone accordion.

So it was incongruous, if somehow inevitable, that a mildly eccentric Perugian would conceive a modern festival celebrating not some ancient Umbrian tradition, but rather that

ultimate American creation: jazz.

Umbria Jazz was founded by Carlo Pagnotta, the festival's artistic director and a man of fine taste who ran a fashionable men's clothing shop in his native Perugia. As crowds promenade along the Corso Cavour, Orvieto's main artery, in dark coats for the festival's winter session, Pagnotta shuffles along in Burberry plaid and a bright yellow vest.

The larger summer festival, held in

Perugia, has featured jazz names like Tony Bennett and Diana Krall, as well as pop stars like Prince and Sting. When it began in 1973, Umbria Jazz was host to then-living masters like Art Blakey, Dizzy Gillespie, and Charles Mingus.

The Hot Language

Later in the evening, the Corso is again calm. Bells ring out from the Torre del Moro every 15 minutes through the quiet streets. It is too late for the restaurants, whose tables are filled for the night, and too early for the bars, which will soon explode with post-dinner congregation.

Inside Gastronomia Arrone, locals fill the few small tables and stand around the salumi counter drinking Orvieto Classico and dipping biscotti into vin santo. Legs of prosciutto hang from the ceiling over wheels of hard cheeses. The proprietor is busy constructing antipasti platters, stopping in his work to salute his customers, most of whom he knows by name.

Two distinguished couples enter together. The women greet friends in the back of the narrow storefront. The men take two recently freed chairs. They order scotch, a drink not commonly consumed by Italians because, as the man with the silver mustache and the light smile in his eye informs, too much impairs the ability to make love.

He is Stefano Cimicchi, former mayor of Orvieto. The summer Umbria Jazz festival in Perugia had been an institution for 20 years when Cimicchi had the wild idea to start a sister festival.

Umbria Jazz Winter was a natural culmination of Cimicchi's love of music, the holiday season, and his hometown. "I was born in Orvieto on Christmas Day," he says, "I play the clarinet. Not

Gil Evans Project performing in the Teatro Mancinelli.

jazz, but philharmonic. Music is very important to me."

Carlo Pagnotta was immediately receptive to Cimicchi's idea. Less enthusiastic was the bishop.

"The bishop and I sat down one night and drank an entire bottle of grappa," says Cimicchi, holding his hand high above the tabletop. "When we finished, the bishop agreed to the concerts, as long as he could give a Mass of peace." Thus from the grapes was born not only Umbria Jazz Winter, but the tradition of the festival's conclusion each New Year's Day with a Mass of peace in the duomo,

followed by a concert of American gospel music.

It was a risk in the hill town notorious for its cold winters. Cimicchi expected a flop, but it was packed. A quarter century on, Cimicchi is especially pleased with the interest in Umbria Jazz he sees among younger generations.

Across town, the small bar area at Il Malandrino Bistrot begins to fill for the all-night jam session. Black and white photographs adorn the walls: Nat King Cole, Miles Davis, Billie Holiday, and the original exile, Sidney Bechet.

Bechet was the first American jazz musician to go to Europe, in 1919. In Paris, he was treated as royalty. Others soon followed in search of artistic appreciation, free from systemic racism.

"The flow of African-American musicians in the 1920s, like Sidney Bechet and Sam Wooding, helped Italian musicians to understand the 'hot' language," says musicologist Stefano Zenni, "Records in Italy were for the elite before World War II. Live performances of American musicians like Louis Armstrong, who played in Turin in 1935, had a fundamental impact."

Pianist Mario Donatone works the room at Il Malandrino between his dinner set and the late-night jam, stopping to greet fans and fellow musicians on his way from the stage to the bar. Like most Italian musicians, he studied classical piano, although he was exposed to American jazz growing up in Rome in the 1960s. "My father was an opera fan, but he owned some records of Louis Armstrong and Duke Ellington, and these musicians were often on Italian television shows," says Donatone.

The American-European experience is an evolving two-way conversation. Jazz is an improvised language distilling disparate voices into a singular expression of self. America is a country of improvisation — multiple peoples mixing around in a constant motion not seen since ancient times, creating a new culture. Jazz was

incubated in New Orleans, where African, European, and Creole traditions entangled in the humid air.

Jelly Roll Morton, a Creole of French ancestry, and his peers developed jazz, in part, from the myriad of styles that found their way to New Orleans. Piano players — Western European, West Indian, white and black — found abundant work behind the keyboards of Storyville brothels. New Orleans at the turn of the 20th century was an explosion of true diversity. "Whatever your tunes were over there, we played them in New Orleans," Morton told Alan Lomax. That is the American paradox — *sui generis*, self-made from all the world.

"Italian jazz musicians are connected with the classical background," Donatone explains. "But my Neapolitan roots give me the soulful feeling, very emotional." When most Americans think of Italian music, they are thinking of the *canzone napoletana* to which Donatone refers, songs like "O Sole Mio." Some of these Italian standards are, in fact, American. Harry Warren (born Salvatore Antonio Guaragna), for example, who composed countless Great American Songbook standards, such as "At Last," "Jeepers Creepers," and "I Only Have Eyes for You," also composed Italian-American standards like "That's Amore" and "Inamorata."

In addition to regional ballads and folk music, it can be argued that opera is the quintessential Italian roots music. The operatic Italian melodrama can be heard not only in Neapolitan ballads and the music of Italian jazz musicians like Donatone, but also in that of Italian-American pop singers from Tony Bennett to Dion DiMucci (note the Puccini-esque introduction to his 1961 pop hit "Runaround Sue").

"Many important Italian jazz musicians revisited the opera music of Puccini and Donizetti. This is a good way for the Italian jazz to find its identity," says Donatone.

And he confirms what musicians —

American and European alike — have struggled with since the first wave of exiles: rhythm.

"As an Italian musician, the biggest difficulty was about the rhythm," says Donatone, "You can learn scales and chords from music books, but the rhythm of jazz was very difficult in the beginning. I learned a lot playing with people better than me."

Donatone echoes earlier American exiles. "Rhythm sections were always a problem then," saxophonist Jay Cameron told Bill Moody, drummer and author of *Jazz Exiles*. "Horn players learned from the records. Rhythm section players ... needed to see how it was done by American drummers."

Long past midnight, Donatone calls four musicians to the stage. They launch into rapid-fire, serious bop. Pianist Giuseppe Vitale rocks back and forth on the bench, shaking the monitors, concealed by his cap to hide his confessed nervousness. Alto Gabriel Marciano and tenor Alex De Lazzari trade choruses, holding the microphone to the other's horn, urging camaraderie over competition. Edoardo Battaglia keeps the madness together behind the drum kit, in frenetic ecstasy.

The players — three Italians and one American — are in high school. They met in Perugia during the summer festival at clinics offered by Berklee College of Music, designed to expose teenagers interested in jazz to an essential in-person immersion. Incredibly, they didn't grow up listening to jazz (although Marciano recalls his father's copy of John Coltrane's *A Love Supreme* in the car), yet they play with reverent, youthful abandon the hardest bop at the festival, blowing well into the wee hours — a native tongue preserved for at least another generation.

Il Jazz Tricolore

There is a quality to the light in Umbria not captured in words or photographs. It faintly filters into the dark streets of the fortified cities, yet it spreads across the rich green countryside in a muted glow, enhancing the morning fog that snakes along the foothills. This light has cultivated some of Italy's finest artists and poets: Giotto, Raphael, Jacopone. Even Umbria's most famous figure, Saint Francis of Assisi — a gentle, spiritual man, known for his deep connection with nature and his communion with the birds and the beasts — was a kind of poet.

This mystical Umbrian light finds its way onto the frescoes of the churches and the tables of the homes and restaurants. There is an Italian word — *sprezzatura* — that describes the Italian ability of turning even minuscule daily tasks into seemingly effortless art. Pasta, for example, that delicate and sublime creation that defines the Italian experience, is nothing more than simple grain — the most basic survival food, transmuted into grace itself.

Bassist Giovanni Tommaso comes from an early generation of Italian jazz pioneers, players once reverently called *senatori*. Tommaso exudes gentle class in thick black frames, a flat cap crowning his long hair, and a blue polka dot tie. The venue for his performances this year at Umbria Jazz, the imposing 14th-century "People's Palace," sits above the Piazza del Popolo. Its height offers a vantage above the rooftops, open to the light cast upon the city walls.

"I felt like Italy was not my ideal place to grow up," says Tommaso, who was born in Lucca in 1941. "I experienced dramatic moments of World War II, like the bombings and my father's deportation by the Germans."

Growing up in occupied, war-torn Italy, Tommaso developed what many Europeans still call the "American Dream." Tommaso recalls the liberation of his hometown — the first time he encountered Americans. "I'll never forget when they were marching in our street in Lucca and one African-American soldier handed me a chocolate bar," he says, "My gratitude for that gesture changed my life."

In a familiar pattern, the young Tommaso's introduction to American culture came from the local cinema. "We didn't have to pay to get in because my friend's father was the administrator," remembers Tommaso, "I loved the American films — Laurel and Hardy, Westerns, and musicals, which were my introduction to standards and consequently to real jazz."

Tommaso has amassed numerous accolades over his long career. But initially he pursued a different kind of education. At the age when most Italian musicians enter conservatory, Tommaso took a gig on a cruise ship.

"In 1959, when I was 18, I left Genoa on the ship *Homeric* sailing to New York," says Tommaso, "At that time New York lived its best era of modern jazz. Two different bands in every club."

His first show was the Miles Davis Quintet at the Apollo. "Listening to that music live was like a shock. That concert, and a few others: the Jazz Messengers with Lee Morgan and Wayne Shorter, Max Roach, Cannonball Adderley. You see, the biggest difference between listening to a record and a live concert is the sound. That can not be reproduced. Listening, watching, and talking to my heroes were my most formative musical experiences."

After cutting his teeth in the jazz clubs of midcentury Manhattan, Tommaso returned to Italy with a unique insight and approach.

"I don't think Italian jazz has a specific musical characteristic," says Tommaso, "but probably a natural melodic vein and a strong instinct toward improvisation."

Tommaso has a theory about Italian musicians' ability for improvisation, both at home and abroad.

"Many of the old musicians were not professionals and only played gigs during weekends," he says. "Self-made musicians must have a good ear and creativity in order to compensate for the lack of technique and musical training.

> **"Listening to [Miles Davis] live was like a shock. ... You see, the biggest difference between listening to a record and a live concert is the sound. That cannot be reproduced. Listening, watching, and talking to my heroes were my most formative musical experiences."**
>
> Giovanni Tommaso

"Many Italian immigrants in America kept the tradition by playing for *feste paesane*, dancing parties and weddings. Probably being exposed to a new world, new people, new music, they grew up musically with more confidence in improvisation."

Between 1880 and 1920, 15 million Italians — mostly from southern Italy — fled their homeland, and the port of New Orleans was a major entry point for Italian immigrants to the New World. The Immigration Act of 1924 expressly limited the number of Italians allowed into the United States. But the one-third of southern Italy already in America by 1920 overcame prejudice to profoundly affect American culture.

"Some of them became very successful jazz musicians, such as Nick La Rocca, who was born in Sicily, the great jazz violinist Joe Venuti, who was born in Como," says Tommaso. "Also Eddie Lang [born Salvatore Massaro], one of the first jazz guitarists."

Tommaso has worked with the true masters, including Sonny Rollins, Dexter Gordon, Gil Evans, Art Farmer, Max Roach, and Kenny Clarke. In 1961, Chet Baker emerged from a Lucca jail on a narcotics rap (speaking perfect Italian). The brooding Oklahoman — whom the Italians called *l'angelo* — put together a combo with Tommaso and toured Italy for six months.

Tommaso's experiences afford him a deep understanding of the continual cultural conversation that is jazz. "I don't like giving geographic labels to jazz styles," he says, "A while ago I wrote a couple of tunes with a *tarantella* groove, a sort of shuffle swing. But that doesn't mean I should call it 'Italian jazz.' "

Tommaso's set at Umbria Jazz is a stunning suite. Accompanied by pianist Rita Marcotulli and drummer Alessandro Paternesi, Tommaso uses three Gershwin songs as a springboard from which to explore his own composition. Just when the listener is consumed by an almost overwhelming harmonic complexity, the trio bursts into an effortless swing, teetering at times on the cusp of tonal anarchy. Marcotulli plucks the strings directly on the piano's soundboard, Tommaso bows the bass, and Paternesi fires off a series of seemingly random rim shots — before tenderly falling into "'S Wonderful," soft and subtle.

An awed silence follows the departing crowd. The piazza below sits in a yellow glow in the still twilight. The sun sinks behind western rooftops, and the music of Tommaso and Gershwin lingers in the chill like currents lapping over Atlantic crossings.

Sweet and Lowdown

Sidney Bechet's exile a century ago continues to inspire new generations. Guitarists Dario Berlucchi's and Alessandro Di Virgilio's musical awakening came while watching Woody Allen's 2011 film *Midnight in Paris*, which features a gypsy jazz soundtrack and Bechet's "Si Tu Vois Ma Mère" as its main theme. They immediately formed a band, Accordi Disaccordi (literally translated as "Agreements Disagreements," they took the name from the Italian translation of *Sweet and Lowdown*, Allen's 1999 film — itself named after a Gershwin song — about a fictional gypsy jazz guitarist living in Django Reinhardt's shadow). Then they took their music to the streets of their native Turin to "bring the music to the people."

Gypsy jazz is the only jazz subgenre of wholly European origin. It is an organic hybrid of European folk music, classical, and jazz, with an emphasis on portable stringed instruments and its own unique rhythm, *la pompe*.

Django Reinhardt, the father of gypsy jazz, was born into the ethnic nomads in

Accordi Disaccordi

Europe called Roma, or Manouches. His caravan was set ablaze one night when a candle accidently landed on the artificial flowers his wife made and sold at cemeteries. Reinhardt was badly burned. With the full use of only two fingers in his disfigured left hand, he was forced to relearn his instrument, fundamentally shaping the sound of European jazz.

Berlucchi and Di Virgilio are not ethnic Gypsies, and make no such claim, but are disciples of the music. "Our music is influenced by the Manouches," says Di Virgilio, "but also by the music of [Argentine guitarist] Gonzalo Bergara. Also, Biréli Lagrène. He does like Django did — mix Manouches with Louis Armstrong and Duke Ellington, but Biréli mixes Django with bebop — another transformation. We try to make something different, to put together all of this."

They call their sound hot Italian swing — playing standards and originals like "Spaghetti Killer" with vivaciousness and a technical proficiency stemming from their conservatory study, which included "everything from Mozart to Django," says Di Virgilio.

"Gypsy jazz is based on an older tradition than even jazz. It is a mixture between classical skills and folk tradition," says Berlucchi. "When I listen to the gypsy, I remember my grandfather. The sound is French-Italian. Django played with accordion players, mixed different sounds and cultures."

"Gypsy jazz is based on swing," adds Di Virgilio. "You can play different harmony, but the tempo, the swing, is the same as 80 years ago."

That swing — *la pompe* — is the backbone of gypsy jazz. While European musicians initially struggle with the nuances of American swing, *la pompe* is an almost sacred indigenous European rhythm.

Among the youngest musicians at Umbria Jazz, Berlucchi and Di Virgilio, accompanied by upright bassist Elia

Lasorsa, are arguably the hardest working, too — playing multiple sets throughout each day, before noon until after midnight. They are first and foremost a street band, and they pride themselves on their ethos of playing anywhere for anyone.

Berlucchi and Di Virgilio were busking on the streets of Perugia during the summer festival when Carlo Pagnotta happened by. He dug what he heard and invited them to play the main stage, making Accordi Disaccordi the only artist to play Umbria Jazz on both the street and as an official act.

"For buskers like us, it is a great honor," says Berlucchi. "Umbria Jazz really makes a dream come true."

The Meaning of the Blues

The lively cobblestone streets in Orvieto's city center are void of sidewalks or painted lines, with scant signage. Pedestrians and cars flow interchangeably in random but cohesive rhythm. An accordion player stands where the two main streets join, his bellowed notes carried in the air down through the Corso and up above the rooftops into the open sky.

Inside Teatro Mancinelli, five levels of private boxes grace the oval hall, drawing one's eye up to the frescoed ceiling and ornate chandelier once lit by candles. The imposing hand-painted curtain depicts the Byzantine general Belisarius freeing Orvieto from the Goths' siege. The 19th-century opera house was not designed for jazz, but this is no ordinary jazz.

Miles Davis was one of the many musicians who congregated at arranger Gil Evans' basement apartment on Manhattan's West 55th Street in the late 1940s. Together they nurtured a new kind of jazz, evidenced on Davis' seminal *Birth of the Cool* and culminating in masterpieces like *Miles Ahead, Porgy and*

Bess, and *Sketches of Spain*.

For the last several years, American arranger and composer Ryan Truesdell has been working with the Evans family to restore Evans' music with unprecedented access to his original charts, resulting in a Grammy-winning album in 2012 (*Centennial: Newly Discovered Works of Gil Evans*) and several special performances. This year at Umbria Jazz, Truesdell and company recreated the Davis-Evans albums *Miles Ahead* and *Porgy and Bess* live in their entirety.

Truesdell conducted a 17-piece band of Italian musicians, augmented by Americans Lewis Nash (drums), Jay Anderson (bass) and Steve Wilson (alto sax), and the Italian trumpeter Paolo Fresu, tackling the seemingly impossible task of recreating Davis' original parts.

Fresu enjoys pop star status in Italy, but he is the exception. Another paradox is that while American jazz musicians once fled to Europe for recognition, European audiences are not necessarily so kind to their own.

"These musicians don't have an easy professional life," says Stefano Zenni, the musicologist. "Jazz has not been really supported in the universities and general culture until recently."

Superstar Fresu received only the second loudest applause, with the most lavished upon drummer Lewis Nash, whose inimitably American rhythm drives the band like a captain at the wheel of a ship at sea. Evans' scores — essentially concertos for trumpet and flugelhorn — weave complex harmonic structure and intricate phrases throughout, propelled by his sly and steady swing.

Evans' jazz has heavy European influences, evidenced in the two suites that make up *Miles Ahead*, from the Spanish folk song "La Paloma Azul," the inspiration for "Blues for Pablo," to the echo of the tone row in Austrian composer Alban Berg's violin concerto that runs throughout "The Meaning of the Blues."

The second half of the program is the *Porgy and Bess* album, Evans' reinterpretation of George Gershwin's American opera. Born to Russian Jewish immigrants in New York's Yiddish Theatre District, Gershwin became the quintessential American composer, writing countless pop standards and much more. Before the minimalism of Philip Glass and Steve Reich in the latter half of the 20th century redefined what is considered American "classical" music, Gershwin envisioned an American classical and opera identity incorporating the indigenous African-American blues, jazz, and ragtime he learned cutting piano rolls alongside stride pianists like James P. Johnson. Much as Frank Lloyd Wright forged a truly new and bold American architecture by embracing America's natural surroundings before being swept away by Bauhaus glass and steel, so too did Gershwin — along with Duke Ellington — successfully fuse orchestral music with the blood and guts of homegrown American blues.

Gershwin's triumph, recast through Evans' and Davis' modernism, translates seamlessly decades and a continent away. "Gil Evans had a great swing," Truesdell says to the mostly Italian audience, "I've performed this piece with other bands where the French horns play it straight." Acknowledging the all-Italian section, he exclaims, "It's so wonderful to hear those swinging French horns!"

At the conclusion of the program, Italian pianist Dado Maroni took the previously vacant Fazioli baby grand to thunderous applause. The band began the loose Gil Evans-composed introduction to Miles Davis' "So What" — based on French composer Claude Debussy's "Voiles" — before kicking into that unmistakable riff and that relentlessly cool and infectious swing.

The incongruity of it all somehow brought everything full circle. The music of a European Jew playing the blues, interpreted through the collaborative genius of two of jazz's greatest voices, one black and one white, whose partnership remains unsurpassed as a free-flowing musical fluency, performed with a mixed band of Italian horns and woodwinds and an American rhythm section, sweetened by the pure phrasing of Italy's greatest jazz star filling the role of American jazz's most eloquent visionary. The opulent Italian opera hall filled effortlessly with the sounds of an opera born ultimately in a Storyville brothel, defined, necessarily, by swing and blues.

Night and Day

Blasts echo through the ancient stone streets like gunfire. Children set off fireworks among the huddled masses gathered in the piazza, flaming bits of shrapnel landing on unsuspecting shoulders. Smoke fills the frenzied piazza as midnight climaxes. When the dust clears, a sole lighted paper candle floats over the duomo.

Songs fill the streets long into the night.

The queue around the cathedral grows an hour before Mass. Only an empty Prosecco bottle in the quiet piazza betrays the madness of the night before. Police pat down parishioners herded through metal detectors at the duomo doors. Inside, two guards stand at every entrance and along the hall, where plastic barriers wall off the central aisle. Orvieto's annual New Year's Day Mass of peace is a potential target for violence in our modern world.

The duomo is itself a paradox. The cathedral for which Orvieto is known is the least Orvietani structure in the city. The materials, forged from volcanic tufa, were imported from distant regions centuries ago; the art inside, the work of Tuscan hands. But Orvieto's pride is just. Built over centuries, the duomo is a spectacular fusion of Italian Gothic and Romanesque architecture, its alternating black and white lines housing sacred relics and magnificent Signorelli frescoes.

Mirroring most medieval city planning, Orvieto's narrow winding streets shield external views, snaking their way through the walled city, depositing the walker into the large and open Piazza del Duomo, as if emerging from a dense forest into a meadow. As one approaches the piazza, the duomo's facade fills the horizon, shimmering pink in illuminated sunlight.

These days, Mass is held in the Corporal Chapel, a tiny enclave more than adequate to serve the diminishing number of worshipers. The large nave is reserved for special occasions, such as Easter, and this, the New Year's Day Mass of peace. But this crowd is here less for salvation than for the show.

The traditional Mass begins in Italian. Suddenly incongruous foreign voices rise in angelic splendor. The American Protestant spiritual "Amazing Grace" fills the cold cathedral. After Mass, Dexter Walker and Zion Movement, a 34-strong gospel choir founded in Walker's grandparents' South Side Chicago basement, begin their set, signifying the conclusion of the Mass of peace, and of Umbria Jazz Winter.

Walker addresses the mostly local crowd: "We have come all the way to Italy from Chicago to celebrate Jesus Christ and praise the Lord," as the choir comes alive with choreography and brightly colored robes to Kool & the Gang's "Celebration." Jubilation pours from the cavernous cathedral, out through the open brass doors, and into the piazza, drifting down Via del Duomo, blending faintly into street guitars and the ever-present chiming of the bells.

Coda

Trattoria dell'Orso is warm and quiet,

Funk Off perform outside Piazza del Duomo.

tucked away in an unassuming side street. The affable proprietor speaks little English and offers quintessential Orvietani fare, including the "Pope's pasta," covered in a mountain of shaved truffles. Truffles grow wild and ubiquitous in Umbria, available to anyone with a dog and the desire to forage.

It is New Year's Day, the closing of the festival and a holy day in Italy. Lewis Nash and his wife are seated at a central table. A local couple enters the small dining room, careful to close the door behind them to keep out the fierce chill. The man recognizes Nash. "Buona serra," he says somewhat timidly and Nash replies with a gracious smile, "buona serra." The man continues in English, "We saw your concert this morning. Thank you for coming here."

It is easy to see the respect jazz musicians have experienced in Europe since Sidney Bechet's first crossing. In this modern world of selfies and live-streaming narcissism, being left alone to one's dinner after a few pleasant words is the ultimate show of respect.

Nash inquires about specials written on a small chalkboard, but the proprietor, after some attempt, is unable to translate. A local patron at the next table explains the menu in a hybrid of English and hand movements. Nash inquires further about a specific sauce, his own hands in motion, as if laying brushes across the skin of a snare.

Christian McBride enters, soon followed by John Patitucci. The bassists and their companions join Nash's table. Dishes soon emerge from the kitchen at regular intervals as the giants of modern jazz rhythm ruminate on the past week's performances — breaking bread over a small wooden table in the center of a small, warm room off a cold and narrow cobblestone street, winding through a fortified medieval city, proudly sitting on a chunk of volcanic rock in the green heart of Italy. ∎

Alison Brown with a Průcha
Banjos Diamond Point model,
which Jarda gave to her in 2002.

Bluegrass in Bohemia

by Alison Brown

THE BANJO JAMBOREE IN Čáslav, Czech Republic, is Europe's oldest bluegrass festival. It's been on my bucket list for years and I finally had the chance to play there last summer on the occasion of its 44th anniversary. Even though I've met a lot of great Czech bluegrass musicians over the years, I was still unprepared for the sheer number of pickers gathered there among the trees. All afternoon and into the evening I heard one great banjo player after another, awestruck that such a uniquely American instrument had found so much love in a country half a world away.

The Czech passion for bluegrass began with the Tramp movement in post-World War I Czechoslovakia. An offshoot of the Boy Scouts, Tramps would go camping in the woods with guitars and tenor banjos, and would sing campfire songs that had roots in American folk music. This Western derivative music subsequently became very popular in Czechoslovakia in the '20s and '30s. During and after World War II, American Armed Forces radio broadcast the sound of Earl Scruggs' bluegrass banjo on Czech airwaves. But it wasn't until Pete Seeger toured Czechoslovakia in 1964 that most people there saw a five-string banjo for the first time. Czech banjo players have described that

as a true eureka moment; before Pete Seeger, most Czechs assumed that Earl Scruggs was somehow flatpicking a tenor banjo.

Keeping the Fire Burning

There have been several important names in the history of Czech bluegrass, but in my opinion, one of the most important these days is Jaroslav Průcha. Jaroslav (he goes by Jarda — the J sounds like a Y) is a master banjo builder, one of the most gifted of his generation, turning out 50 exquisitely made banjos each year from a small workshop nestled in the suburbs of Prague. He grew up in the '60s and '70s against the backdrop of com-munism and the Russian occupation, and his journey to becoming one of the world's greatest contemporary banjo makers seems to have happened in spite of such odds. It almost reads like a fairy tale.

After the Russians invaded Czechoslovakia in 1968, American bluegrass, folk, and country music were forbidden as symbols of Western culture. But that oppression made the Czech passion for bluegrass burn even brighter. Families that could no longer vacation outside of the country would spend their holidays at campgrounds, keeping the spirit of the Tramp movement alive as they sang American bluegrass songs

around the campfire.

In a fascinating twist, while bluegrass music in America and its nostalgia for the past could be considered con-servative, the same music took on a revolutionary meaning in the hearts of the Czech people.

"When the Russians came, my father was very upset," Jarda recalls. "But for me, scouting, music, and freedom were in my heart anyway. Once we were camping in the trees and a band came to visit us. Four musicians — guitar, bass, fiddle and ... banjo ... four string, but banjo! They brought this nice music, bluegrass, which helped people here to feel freedom in their hearts, even if it was only for the weekend while they were sitting by the fire, singing, playing guitars and banjos. This music brought people together. It made a protest to the government and let people say through the words of the songs what they loved and wanted, and to show the government we can be happy. From that time I had the sound of the banjo [in] my mind all the time."

When Jarda was 14, he bought a black market copy of Earl Scruggs' instruc-tional book from a classified ad in the back of a newspaper. The book had been translated into the Czech language and had no photos, just tablature and text. Jarda worked his way through it using a set of picks that he hand cut from a tin can, boiling them with chemicals from a hardware store to nickel plate the raw stainless steel.

"Every afternoon when I came home from school, I would practice the tunes in my Scruggs book," he says. "Every day, all weekend, again and again. ... The only thing that could stop me from playing my banjo was when my father would turn the electricity off in my room at night so he could go to sleep!"

Luboš Malina, a Czech banjo virtuoso, told me that in the 1970s it was nearly impossible to buy a good five-string banjo. Luboš is a founding member of Druhá Tráva. Their progressive bluegrass sound, fueled by lead singer/poet Robert Křesťan, became the soundtrack for the Velvet Revolution in 1989. The group achieved the popularity of rock stars in the Czech Republic and built an international reputation through relentless worldwide touring once the border to the West opened.

"The only way to get a five-string banjo," says Luboš, "was to buy it in West Germany and bring it home — which was very difficult and dangerous too — or [you could] build it yourself. So some musicians started building banjos."

Banjo Beginnings

Jarda spent the equivalent of half a month's salary to buy his first five-string banjo. It was a homemade affair with a modified guitar neck and a rim made out of stainless steel sheet metal. A year later, he was able to upgrade to a Marma banjo from East Germany, but he could tell from photos that it wasn't made to the same specs as the banjos that the American players used. Thus, he was driven to make his first banjo. That was in 1974 and he remembers clearly how excited he felt as he built it — he knew he was on to something very special.

Jarda finished school a few years later, having studied precision machinery. His trade, coupled with his passion for the banjo, found a perfect

marriage in the launch of Průcha Banjos.

He explains that instrument making and machining trades both have a long tradition in the Czech Republic, so, in his mind, the existence of a world-class banjo workshop in Prague is more than a happy accident.

Putting his professional training to work, Jarda began making all the metal parts for his banjos. He's unique in that way; no other banjo maker in the world also manufactures all the metal components. So it was natural that, over time, Průcha Banjos' business has expanded to supplying parts for many American banjo makers as well.

In 1989, after the Velvet Revolution and with the fall of communism, Jarda visited the US for the first time. He and a friend arrived in New York with just $350 in their pockets and two banjos to sell to underwrite their six-week visit. Some American friends took pity on them and bought month-long Greyhound passes for the pair. They immediately headed to Owensboro, Kentucky, for the International Bluegrass Music Association's World of Bluegrass convention.

Jarda remembers that trip as like being in heaven. It was there that he met Geoff Stelling, founder of Stelling Banjos, for the first time. Before he left the Czech Republic, Jarda had made a replica of a Stelling Staghorn banjo, going only by the knowledge that the banjo head was 11 inches in diameter and from looking at the photos in their catalog. When Geoff examined the banjo Jarda created, he was amazed to see that the only variance in the dimensions was a one-millimeter difference in the size of the headstock. When Jarda explained that he had cut all the shell inlays from a raw shell by hand, Geoff was even more amazed — so much so that he offered Jarda a job working at Stelling Banjos. Though Jarda was interested, the opportunity was ultimately sidelined when the American Embassy refused to grant Jarda a work visa. That was a big

disappointment, but it kept Jarda focused on building his business in Prague.

Partnering with two other machinists, he developed and built tone rings (which Jarda describes as the soul of the banjo) as well as tension hoops and flanges. This expertise positioned Průcha to become a worldwide supplier of banjo parts and, in 2000, he won a huge contract to supply all the banjo and mandolin parts for Gibson. Other banjo makers followed Gibson's lead, and Průcha Banjos' growing business supported the acquisition of a CAD

Alison Brown at the Banjo Jamboree in Čáslav.

design system. That 3D modeling technology has enabled Jarda to build some of the best-playing banjo necks being made today.

No Translation Needed

More than 40 years since Jarda made his first banjo, he continues to dig deep into his craft, looking for ways to improve his instruments and make a contribution to the global banjo community. On a recent trip to North Carolina, he purchased the flange and tension hoop from a prewar Gibson banjo — a very expensive bit of R&D. He studied the pot's metal composition and invested in the machinery to recreate the one-piece flange. The initial reaction of the banjo obsessives to his latest innovation is one of amazement.

I asked Jarda if he ever looks back on the path his life has taken and wonders how it might have all worked out differently if it hadn't been for the banjo. He told me: "When I hear that instrument, banjo — which is still out of tune, makes very loud noise, is very heavy, ... I love it, play it, it is my job. I can make a living from it knowing that I won't be rich but it gives me enough. Through the banjo and this music, I meet so many good people who speak the same language and no one needs to translate it — nice music, coming from our hearts."

How the song of the banjo can touch so many hearts, across so many continents, is something that will never cease to inspire wonder in me. Truly, all banjo players can celebrate the fact that America's instrument has also inspired so many beyond our borders, and can be thankful that, against all odds, Jarda Průcha heeded the banjo's call. ■

Instruments of the world

In the West, we've become so accustomed to seeing roots musicians strumming a six-string (often acoustic) guitar, we'd be forgiven for thinking such an instrument is the queen of the jungle. But guitars can have anywhere from four to eighteen strings, and the origins of the guitar stretch deep into European and Iberian history, making it one among countless stringed instruments that are used for playing traditional music worldwide. In the following pages are merely a handful of other stringed instruments used frequently in the roots music of other parts of the world.

— **Kim Ruehl**
Illustrations by Drew Christie

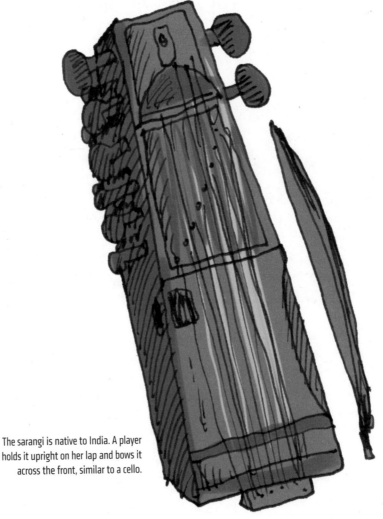

The sarangi is native to India. A player holds it upright on her lap and bows it across the front, similar to a cello.

The yueqin, or moon lute, is a
traditional Chinese instrument held
and played with a pick like a Western
guitar or mandolin.

The erhu, or two-stringed Chinese fiddle, is native to
China. The player bows between the strings and the neck.

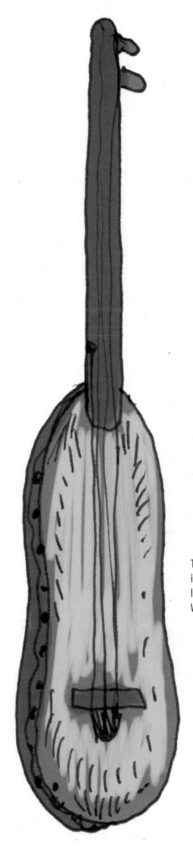

The ngoni is a plucked lute-like instrument played across one's lap like a guitar. It is prevalent throughout West Africa.

The kora is a West African instrument, masterfully popuarlized by Toumani Diabaté. The player holds the two handles with the strings facing him, and strums with his thumbs.

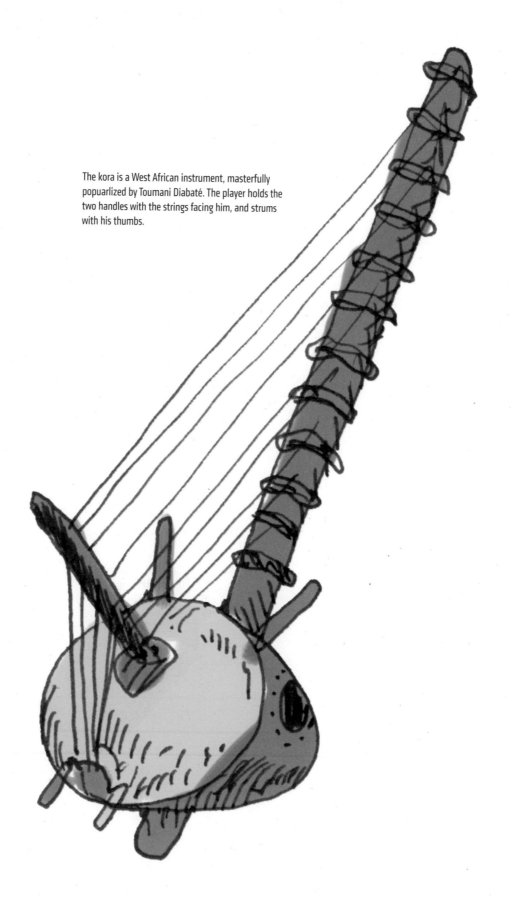

The rubab originated in Afghanistan and is held across one's lap like a guitar.

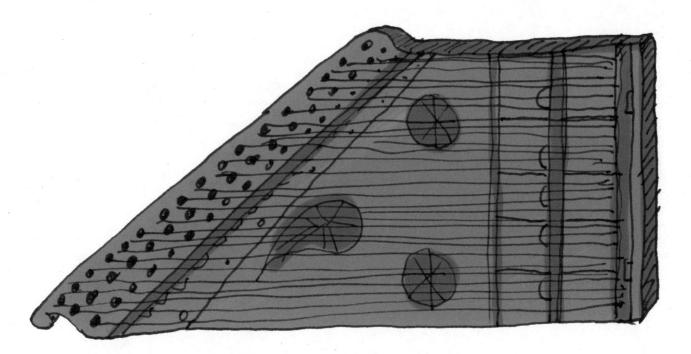

The qanun looks similar to a hammered dulcimer, but is picked and strummed like a harp or guitar. It is prevalent in the Middle East, West Africa, and Central Asia.

REMAINING IN LIGHT

A conversation with Angélique Kidjo

by Megan Romer

ANGÉLIQUE KIDJO HAS been defying the boundaries of so-called "world music" since her first recordings. She's collaborated with a long, diverse list of artists that includes Ziggy Marley, Josh Groban, Alicia Keys, Carlos Santana, and plenty of others. Her solo records bear the influences of Afro-pop, jazz, gospel, R&B, rock, and the traditional musics of her native Benin.

Her most recent project is a large-scale Carnegie Hall concert to be recorded this May and set for release later in 2017, in which she covers the entire 1980 Talking Heads new-wave/post-punk/Afro-funk opus *Remain in Light*.

We recently talked over the phone before her Zumba class about that Talking Heads album, lessons she learned from her father, and what it's been like for her to be in America lately.

MEGAN ROMER: This interview started with kind of a funny coincidence. I was assigned the piece by my editor on Inauguration Day, Jan. 20. The next day was the Women's March [Jan. 21], and I was watching at home. There wasn't a march near me and it didn't work to travel, so I had it streaming on my computer. I got up and left the room with it still running, and I was in the kitchen making tea and heard the opening strains of Sam Cooke's "A Change Is Gonna Come." I got excited because that's one of my favorite songs, and I came running into the living room to see who was singing it — and it was you! And I was so excited! I mean, I had just been catching up on everything you've done lately and listening to your music, since the interview was on my mind. But I was particularly excited to see you onstage at the march because I was worried that there wouldn't be adequate representation of women of color, let alone African women.

ANGÉLIQUE KIDJO: Yes! Oh, it was so wonderful. I was actually the first performer to be invited to be at the Women's March, and of course I said yes. It was so important to do that; to bring people together to stand up for what is right.

Standing in solidarity with so many other women from all walks of life, and representing African women on that stage, was very powerful. And performing was wonderful.

"A Change Is Gonna Come" was really such a meaningful song for that performance. That song is from 1964, and it is so relevant today! All of the issues it talks about, they are all still going on. Can you believe it?

I took my daughter to Obama's inauguration. I felt we had to go, we had to see. It was such an amazing moment in history, to be there, and to see that. It was such a positive moment.

Singing that song was also a positive moment, to be honest with you. That song, it reminds me so much of the music I grew up on: soul, rhythm and blues, you know. I have always loved so many kinds of music from all over the world. I grew up listening to many things. My father always told us that the world does not stop at our doorstep. [He taught us how] understanding many different cultures would help us to understand our own culture, and the world at large. So yeah, I have always enjoyed music from all over, every genre, it doesn't matter. I like good music, and good music is everywhere. That's part of the reason I am so excited about my upcoming Carnegie Hall performance!

The first time I came to New York in 1992 to play a concert at S.O.B.'s, do you know who came? It was David Byrne. And he loved it. And I have to be honest, I didn't exactly know that David Byrne was part of the Talking Heads. [Laughs.] But I really

"Humanity does the same things over and over. Sometimes we never learn."

Angélique Kidjo

loved their records and thought they were so innovative and interesting!

That album, *Remain in Light,* so much of it comes from studying a book called *African Rhythm and African Sensibility*, by John Miller Chernoff. They really, really studied African music to make that album. I think to myself, "Oh, I've gotta bring this back!" And we're really, really having fun doing it. It's going to be a great time.

MR: It must be fun to just dig in and play some rock and roll, huh?

AK: Oh, it's so much fun. I mean, I have fun performing, always, and like I said, I see no real boundaries between styles of music. But these songs, they are so much fun. And they are really, very meaningful. These songs are still totally relevant to this world. ... They can be applied to everything that is going on in the world today. Not just the United States — all over the world.

MR: *Remain in Light* is from 1980, which was a year that was politically very similar to this one here in the United States, right? A liberal president had just left office, and a new conservative populist celebrity had been elected. There was a lot of racial tension, poverty issues were coming to light, women's issues ...

AK: Exactly! It all just goes in cycles,

doesn't it? Humanity does the same things over and over. Sometimes we never learn. We just keep doing [the same things]. But it's okay, because it gives us the chance to keep learning and keep working.

MR: Yeah, I mean, I kind of like fighting, honestly. I might be disappointed if I had nothing to fight for.

AK: [Laughs] Yes! Me too! Me too. As long as you keep fighting for the good things, that's what matters. Be on the right side.

MR: Speaking of that, I just got a CD in the mail called *République Amazone* from a project called "Les Amazones d'Afrique," and there you are! You're part of this group. And this CD is raising money for the Panzi Foundation, which provides support to women who were victims of domestic violence in the Congo, right?

AK: Yeah, exactly, you've got it. This is a really fun project, many African women from all over are part of it. ... It's so nice to be a part of projects like this.

MR: You're part of a lot of them! I mean, over the years, I think I've gotten maybe five or six million different albums that have featured Angélique Kidjo raising awareness or funds for an amazing project or organization dedicated to African women or women around the world.

AK: [Laughs] Yes! I love to lend my voice. You know, the situation in Africa is complicated, and different in different places [on the continent], but when it comes down to it, African women have to stand up for African women, because we are the only ones who can. I'm in a position to do that, so for me, it is very clear. I have to be doing what we all should be doing! It is right to do what is right, you know?

MR: So it isn't a sort of thing where people are pressuring you all the time? No guilt trips for you?

AK: No, no pressure here. No one's going to pressure me. If I don't want to do something, I'm not going to do it. I do projects I love, because when I commit to a project, I commit all the way. I put all of my energy into it.

My father always taught us this: there is no guilt in this house. If you do something wrong, you apologize, and you move on. If the person doesn't want your apology, forget it, just move on. Don't live with guilt. Guilt is a hole that you dig for yourself and you never get out of. Everything you do, you always feel guilty about it.

MR: Your father sounds like an awfully wise man.

AK: Oh, yeah. He realized early on in

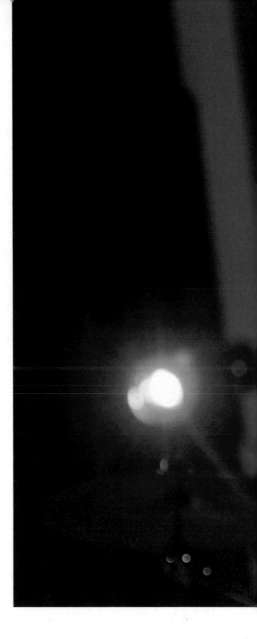

"**When it comes down to it, African women have to stand up for African women, because we are the only ones who can. It is right to do what is right, you know?**"
Angélique Kidjo

his life what is important and what is not, and his family was more important than anything else — his girls, his boys. And he wanted his kids to be able to live in this world. He wanted us to be able to challenge ourselves, and challenge other people. He doesn't believe in color, he doesn't believe in division or violence. ... He has zero patience for racism. When he'd hear someone talking like this, he'd say, "Get out of my house. You used to be welcome here, but now you're no longer welcome here, don't come back."

MR: I know there's always this idea that you can talk to people about their bigotries and convince them to do what's right, but I just don't want bigots in my house. There's no right answer but I don't think bigots are welcome to my company. I mean, I'm great! I'm fun to be around! If you want to be a racist, you don't get to spend time with me.

AK: [Laughing] Yes, me too! Nuh-uh,

that's it!

I mean, one thing I took away from my mother that I use all the time, if people hate you? Kill them with kindness. Because that's a weapon they can't do nothing about!

MR: The political situation in this country is very uncomfortable right now, really from both sides, but in particular there is a lot of policy being passed right now that is directly targeted at immigrants. Do you feel particularly concerned or threatened, as an immigrant yourself and someone who works with international communities?

AK: Well, I think we all have to chill and see how this is going to unfold for the country and for the world. Panicking is not a solution. Let's be logical, lawful, and deal with this. We have rules and we have laws in this country. As an immigrant in this country, and as an American — I have an American passport — I'm fighting for

everybody's rights to have a better life, to have a better quality of life, all over the world.

If we have a world that is more fair and more equal, people won't have to migrate somewhere else. Leaving another country is so painful, when you do it because something bad happened. You can't put yourself in the shoes of somebody who has left home searching for security, safety, everything, when you don't know what is going to happen, what tomorrow is going to be. For any human being, that is a trauma.

So I think we ought to really be careful what we do and what we say to each other, because we belong to each other! There's only one humanity, and we are linked and intertwined. I am always hopeful. If [humans] hadn't been so resilient in surviving, we wouldn't be here today. Violence

and hating other people is not the solution. It is just a dead end. It takes too much of your energy away. It does nothing. And fear does [nothing], too, and cowardice.

MR: Yeah, I don't know how to help people be less afraid of each other, but I think that has to be the goal, really.

AK: I mean for me, all these issues, I find that I can use music to talk about them in a positive way. In May, this concert [the Carnegie Hall performance of *Remain in Light*] is going to be dedicated to everyone in the room, to tell them that we can remain in light. We can keep this fight going on until we regain our freedom and our rights, and then to keep them!

I listen to this album, and it's just amazing, the messages in there, and I think it's going to resonate with people, and they'll say, "Well, remaining in light is the way to go!" ■

Krishna Das plays harmonium during a kirtan.

ANYTHING CAN BE A TEMPLE

Through ancient music, bhakti kirtan teaches many to silence their mind

by Justin Joffe

> **"When we get into a room with each other and are singing, that's the thread on which all the beads of the mala are strung."**
> Nina Rao

WEDGED BETWEEN A tattoo parlor and a home appliance store on 1st Avenue in Manhattan, the Bhakti Center leaves its side entrance unlocked for Thursday night kirtan.

Inside, people grab floor cushions and bow to a life-sized statue of A.C. Bhaktivedanta Swami Prabhupada, founder of the International Society of Krishna Consciousness, or ISKCON. His devotees are perhaps better known as orange-robed, tambourine-toting Hare Krishnas.

Prabhupada founded ISKCON in 1966, when he first visited Tompkins Square Park in New York City's East Village and introduced the Free Love generation to bhakti yoga — a practice of absolute love and devotion to God. Under the park's elm tree, Prabhupada first introduced Americans to the Maha Mantra (Hare Krishna), and the tree still reminds practitioners of his presence. At the nearby Bhakti Center, a high definition television reminds me of the center's status among ISKCON ashrams when "#homecourtadvantage" appears on the screen.

There, two smiling yogis stand with a plate of cookies at the bottom of the stairs that lead guests up to a temple on the third floor. Upstairs, a small shrine in the center of the room depicts the adolescent Krishna — an ancient Hindu deity — meeting his beloved Radha in the Vrindavan forest, playing his flute for her as they profess their devotion to each other. A young woman in a leopard print sweater kneels on the floor on a cushion, close to the shrine, beside a white-haired, older man in khakis. Another woman, covered head-to-toe in intricate tattoos, puts her cushion down in front of mine, sits, and starts slowly rocking back and forth.

Incense floods my nostrils as the kirtan begins: a drummer hits a khol drum, someone pumps the harmonium organ, and we roll into the practice, singing "Hare Krishna" again and again.

Planting New Seeds

While the word "yoga" likely calls to mind a room full of people standing in the same pose, the practice of pose-striking (asana) is just one of yoga's eight "limbs," or practices, that can guide a person toward enlightenment. Other "limbs" include breathing practices, behaviors and beliefs like purity and nonviolence, and then there is dharana, or concentration. One way to quiet the mind and concentrate on dharana is to chant a mantra or the name of a deity, using a mala (a similar idea to Catholic rosary beads). There is an array of approaches to dharana, and among them is singing kirtan.

Kirtan is a musical form based on call-and-response group singing. The styles most popular in the US are frequently focused on narratives about gods and prophets, though occasionally it's merely the repetition of a single figure's name. Regardless of what style of kirtan one sings, its hypnotic, repetitive melodies and rhythms — often accompanied by instruments like sitar, tabla drums, harmonium, and occasionally, in the States, acoustic guitar — are aimed at quieting the mind and bringing its participants closer to their spiritual center. Granted, most styles of music are capable of both those things, but for kirtan those are the clearly

established primary objectives. Not unlike the call-and-response singing that's traditional in American folk and church hymns — and the variations that have proliferated throughout country, bluegrass, pop, and other American music styles — kirtan is deeply rooted in Indian tradition. Yet a handful of artists like White Sun, Krishna Das, Jai Uttal, Prince Rama, and others have found ways to introduce this traditional Indian music and its accompanying yogic culture to Western audiences in ways that Americans can both understand and make their own.

In the bhakti yoga tradition, kirtan can pull from a slew of different regional, devotional, sung chanting practices. There are as many different types of kirtan as there are villages in India. However, many Westerners don't realize this, as the differences have largely been homogenized and masked by the way kirtan is described and practiced stateside.

Here in the US, where the sacred music of countless religions and belief systems mingles in cities like New York, participatory kirtans from the Bengali tradition of Vaishnavist Hinduism are the most popular of the genre, incorporating stories from poet-saints in worship to deities like Vishnu, Rhada Krishna, Ramà, Hanuman, and others.

Before Prabhupada founded ISKCON, a style of performance-based kirtan was brought here by the Bengali saint Paramahansa Yoganada, who sang the guru Nanak Dev's Hay Hari Sundara with 3,000 people at Carnegie Hall in 1923. But in the 50 years since ISKCON was founded, 500 temples have sprung up, along with a veritable cottage industry around bhakti yoga.

This yogic practice — with all eight of its limbs — has spread across the world with gatherings, or satsangs, like Bhakti Fest, which draws thousands of practitioners annually to Joshua Tree, California. And, despite the deep

Prince Rama

"We were a generation that recognized there were deeper realities. The problem is that we didn't recognize that in order to change the world, we had to change ourselves. And that was much harder. Nothing in our upbringing or our culture really prepared us for looking within in a new way."

Krishna Das

tradition of kirtan in India, its story, and that of ISKCON and bhakti yoga, is a peculiarly American-like story, wherein centuries of similar but separate traditions are synthesized into an all-encompassing new culture. But digging into the roots of kirtan, one has to wonder: Is anything lost when the devotional aspects fade to the background?

'Whatever Gets You There'

Indian spiritual leaders have sung kirtan naked in the mountains for centuries, and the Sikhs have a huge kirtan tradition, borne from the same bhakti revolution that brought devotional chanting to the lower castes of Northern India during the Middle Ages and took on an entirely new life in Los Angeles. Buddhist monastic chanting developed in a similar vein to kirtan, and a separate Sufi Muslim kirtan tradition eventually emerged as well. But there's something about the bhakti practice that has resonated particularly strongly with Americans.

Taraka Larson, who makes up one half of the futurist "Now Age" art pop duo Prince Rama with her sister Nimai, grew up in Texas with Hare Krishna parents before moving to Alachua, Florida, the largest ISKCON community in the United States, when she was 16.

"My parents converted to the Hare Krishna faith back in the '60s, in the very early days," she says. "They didn't even have such a thing as dhotis, they would just get bed sheets, dye them orange with the closest color to saffron that they could, and that's what they would wear. There

were no yoga classes, no soy milk."

When I ask if she considers the Bhakti Center in the East Village a proper ISKCON temple, she challenges my reasoning. "Anything can be a temple," she says. "When I first moved to New York City, I really gravitated towards Times Square. When you have such sensory overload, your mind almost shuts off and it becomes blank. Whatever gets you there, you know?"

Prince Rama's songs, particularly those on their 2010 album *Shadow Temple*, blur the line between pop music and mantra. The Larson sisters understand that a pop song, with its repetitive verses and chorus, has a similar effect on the mind and body to chanting, and Taraka Larson's views on kirtan offer a window into how that practice can take on different shapes and colors.

That is also something to which Krishna Das can attest. A Grammy-winning, New York-based kirtan artist and one of the most beloved musicians in the bhakti yoga community, Krishna Das folds Western chords and song structures into his kirtan practice, while chanting all names of God, not just those worshipped by the Vaishnavists.

He likes to share a quote from Saint John of the Cross: "In the beginning, the Father uttered one word. That word is his Son, and he utters him forever in everlasting silence. And it is in silence that the heart must hear."

"So this is the Om," he explains. "The first vibration of creation is a sound, and that sound is uttered forever in silence. Silence is the space beyond thought. It's not the crushing of thought, because you can't crush thoughts."

"Sometimes the head and the heart, they don't really go together," echoes Larson. "But it's all about creating that synergy, right? I think that's the kirtan rule, in a way. It's creating a new rhythm, because thoughts are just rhythms."

To that end, kirtan may require vulnerability, but practicing it eventually transforms that vulnerability into strength. It's an exercise for the mind, the body, and the heart — all at once — and it has to start with silence.

"You can't think yourself out of a prison that's made of thought," Krishna Das tells me.

Two hours later, I grab my shoes and leave the Bhakti Center, where any intention to keep some distance in the interest of objective reporting has been silenced through singing kirtan.

Songs for Everyone

Sometime after the 12th century, a bhakti movement spread north from South India. It wasn't until four centuries later, though, when a spiritual leader named Chaitanya Mahaprabhu founded Gaudiya Vaishnavism, interpreting the Bhagavad Gita scripture to teach that bhakti marga — the way of loving devotion to God — was a path to spiritual enlightenment.

Chaitanya's followers worshiped him as Krishna. They extolled his teaching of kirtan, which introduced them to texts that had previously only been available to the highest caste of Brahmins, and only in Sanskrit. During this bhakti revolution, other poet-saints also emerged, bringing their interpretations of the Sanskrit texts to the common people, taking key concepts and inserting them into digestible, narrative-based songs and poems.

"In the old days, those who chanted were the priests, and they chanted in Sanskrit," explains Nina Rao, Krishna Das' longtime friend, business manager, and fellow kirtan leader. "You would only know Sanskrit if you had time to study it. Most people had no time to study it because they were busy tending the fields. Some of them couldn't read, they could only speak the colloquial language."

Making these old, traditional songs available to just anyone was a radical idea at the time, because it challenged India's caste system, allowing practitioners of lower castes to congregate in satsang.

"The caste system isn't just a mark of social identity, but it has economic implications as well," says Eben Graves, a Columbia University ethnomusicologist who has studied kirtan in depth. "If you're a Brahmin, you're supported by other castes economically, so you can do your ritual activities."

Indeed, many 19th century movements in Bengal were supported by landed elites, who offered practitioners patronage to make music. In the 20th century, some musicians became involved in the commercial music industry, but it was still the traveling performers back in Bengal who made a solid living from performing live.

"Today you have [kirtan] musicians who sign contracts, who say, 'I'm going to come perform at your temple in May and I need 8,000 rupees,'" Graves says. "But you can find this in the West, too. I've been to plenty of kirtans that are donation-only, while others are 10 dollars to get in the door."

Of course, when different musical styles traverse the globe, they're not only moving between different systems of meaning, but also through different economic systems. Though some people might bristle at the idea of charging money to sing spiritual music, a look at the history of ISKCON through this frame clears some of the negative stigma surrounding organizations and kirtans that ask for money.

"It came from this Colonial period, and there was always this kind of nationalist impulse to it," says Graves. "The original people who set off in this direction [of spreading kirtan] were elites in Calcutta working for the British government, and they were trying to carve out their own identity as Indians through their religion, so they took these really militant stances about who they were religiously and devotionally. It's very easy to look at proselytization as them just trying to make money, but if you trace back the genealogy of it, it's really rooted in this rethinking of what their devotional tradition was."

Less vindicated by historical context is the harmonium — the pump organ at the heart of kirtans both Eastern and Western since its introduction to Asia in the first half of the 20th century.

"During the Indian independence movement, both British and Indian scholars condemned the harmonium for embodying an unwelcome foreign musical sensibility," writes Matt Rahaim in "That Ban(e) of Indian Music: Hearing Politics in the Harmonium," an article from a 2011 edition of *The Journal of Asian Studies.*

"It was consequently banned from All-India Radio from 1940 to 1971, and still is only provisionally accepted on the national airwaves. The attempt to banish the sound of the harmonium was part of an attempt to define a national sound for India, distinct from the West. Its continued use in education served a somewhat different national project: to standardize Indian music practice."

Conversely, Graves suggests, "People accept the exoticism of South Asia or India through the timbre of musical instruments. If you go to see a musical performance and there's a tabla, for example, that stands for an authenticity of India even if the tabla isn't playing any pattern that's recognizable as a metric."

Taking Root

In 1967, exiled from Harvard University with his colleague Timothy Leary after their famed LSD experiments got a little too groovy, a man named Richard Alpert traveled to India, met another American seeker, Kermit Michael Riggs (soon to become the spiritual singer and teacher known as Bhagavan Das), and eventually found Maharaj-ji.

The guru Maharaj-ji, or Neem Karoli Baba, was responsible for teaching many American seekers to sing all names of god at his Kainchi Dham ashram in the Himalayas. It was there that Alpert became Ram Dass, Jeffrey Kagel became Krishna Das, and a musician named Douglas Uttal become the kirtan artist Jai Uttal.

In 1971 Ram Dass extolled his teachings with his iconic book of mandalas and mantras, *Be Here Now,* turning an entire generation on to the

Jai Uttal

school of American folk music. Uttal played the banjo as a child, and after discovering kirtan at one of Central Park's "Be-Ins," he headed to the West Coast to study the sarod — a classical Indian stringed instrument — with virtuoso Ali Akbar Khan.

Indeed, they were two of many travelers who spent several years searching in India — The Beatles arrived in Rishikesh to study with Maharishi Mahesh Yogi a year after Krishna Das and Uttal first met Maharij-ji. And, at different points, both felt as though they couldn't sing anymore. They became consumed by drug and alcohol abuse, seeking fleeting intimacy over absolute devotion, and deeply troubled by concerns about their mounting fame as kirtan leaders.

In the West, says Uttal, "kirtan gets mixed up with very Western concepts such as celebrity, popularity, fame, and money. I see it in some of my students, I see it at the big festivals, I see it in myself. And that's where my own work is: To not deny that those things exist, but always go to the deeper place that resides within."

Krishna Das echoes this. "People from my generation wanted to change the world," he says. "We were a generation that recognized there were deeper realities. The problem is that we didn't recognize that in order to change the world, we had to change ourselves. And that was much harder. Nothing in our upbringing or our culture really prepared us for looking within in a new way. That's why a lot of the impulses that started a lot of cultural movements kind of fell apart, because of the self-centeredness of each person in those movements."

Thus, it's been through chanting and singing the names of the gods and goddesses that these white, American men began to learn how complete surrender could became a fortifying, strengthening presence in their lives.

When I ask him to explain this, Krishna Das starts with our mutual understanding about the name of God in

practice of chanting.

Ram Dass likes to tell the story of trying to trip out Maharaj-ji on the "yogi medicine" LSD, but says Maharaj-ji acted exactly the same on the drug as he did sober. Krishna Das often recalls what Maharaj-ji told him about the experience: "LSD puts you in the room with Christ, but you can't stay."

"It's good for beginners," Krishna Das tells me, "and we're all beginners. We're attached to our bodies, we identify with

our emotions and our thoughts — that's the definition of a beginner. So pharmacology helps us see through that.

"How we're going to live in a new place," he adds, "now that takes some work."

Though Krishna Das and Jai Uttal share the same guru, Uttal's kirtans add colors from musical styles like reggae and Brazilian bossa nova or samba into his practice, while Krishna Das pulls more from the James Taylor and Paul Simon

the Torah, through a lens of the Jewish faith he and I were both born into, as an unpronounceable sound. I ask him how he connects that bit of Judaic theology to his practice.

His answer: "The true name can never be spoken because it's not a concept in the mind. The true name is presence, the true name is silence, the true name is reality. The true name is not a thought, not a word, not even a sound. It's silence. It's beyond anything that the human mind or intellect or emotions can feel.

"Maharaj-ji once said, 'Go on, sing your lines, fake, false Ram Ram! One of these days you'll say it right.' We're just practicing."

Then he adds, "This is not something that's useful to dwell on intellectually too much. The fruit of practice is realization, inside — knowing in a new and deeper way."

Wide Appeal

Adjunct from ISKCON's practices, Maharaj-ji's teachings took the same stories and participatory kirtans into a less regional, more universal idea of God. But some other important seeds were planted toward the end of the '60s, too.

A Sikh known as Yogi Bhajan brought his brand of kundalini yoga from Punjab to Los Angeles in 1969, with his nonprofit Healthy, Happy, Holy Organization, or 3HO. Kundalini yoga focuses on the energy (shakti) that resides at the base of the spine, and posits that awakening that energy will lead one to enlightenment. Yogi Bhajan merged kundalini yoga with tantric mantras that were quickly rejected by orthodox Sikhs back home. Nonetheless, his style of kundalini is taught in yoga schools all over the country, and kundalini-devotee music group White Sun won the Best New Age album at the 2017 Grammy Awards for their kirtan recording, *White Sun II*.

White Sun singer Gurujas says that the group started soon after she first met her teacher, Hari Jiwan Singh Khalsa, a prominent American Sikh and disciple of Yogi Bhajan, in 2005.

"Hari Jiwan started White Sun to bring the mantras of yogic technology, of yogic science to a larger audience," says Gurujas. "The yogic science is over 5,000 years old, and experiential-based. Every action promotes a reaction, and that's why we chant the mantra. They affect the way that neurons fire in the brain, they affect the gray matter of the brain, and the velocity of the neurons."

Gurujas also says that White Sun's style of kirtan doesn't have a belief system, and that Yogi Bhajan's brand of yogic science doesn't require one — perhaps its nondenominational nature is what has caused White Sun to appeal to such a wide audience. The yoga classes Gurujas teaches at places like the Rama Institute in Venice, California, are largely about pressing play and being present with other practitioners.

"Somebody asked me to initiate them and I didn't even know what they were talking about," she says. "You just put the CD on, listen to it, and see what happens."

By focusing less on the participatory practice of physically producing sounds live in a room, Gurujas liberates her brand of kundalini yoga from the associations of spiritual congregation that follow bhakti practitioners. Meanwhile, her scientific approach to understanding the effects that mantras have on the self is more appealing to her students — and more practical — than those aimed at the heart. Of course, when devotional practice and spirituality are out of the picture, it's natural to wonder if other motives might come into play.

"You always have to think of the subjectivity of who's speaking, right?" asks Eben Graves. "I see this as much with my work in Bengal as with someone like Krishna Das and Jai Uttal, because they always have to think about their career as a musician, about going places to perform and attracting a lot of people. And this is why there's so much apprehension, historically, about the exchange of money involved with music, especially devotional music: What's guiding the performance?"

Pulled In

Whether it's White Sun's non-denominational kirtan or Krisha Das's spirit-centered practice, Sridhar Silberfein embraces all paths to devotional love equally. Based out of the Center for Spiritual Studies in Santa Monica, California, he began thinking about creating something called Bhakti Fest in 1969, when he produced Swami Satchidananda's onstage invocation to the audience at Woodstock. "He looks out at the crowd and I say, 'Someday we're going to have this many people chanting the names of God,'" Silberfein recalls. "Forty years later, almost to the day, was the first Bhakti Fest."

That inaugural event, in 2009, drew more than 1,000 people, and has only grown since. The vegetarian, sober festival presents all modalities of yoga, including physical practice such as asana and dance among its kirtans. Bhakti Fest is, perhaps, the largest such gathering each year in North America, so it's not surprising that it has its doubters.

Krishna Das' manager Nina Rao says that such events initially made her uncomfortable. "The first time I went to Bhakti Fest I literally got there and said to my friend, 'I've got to leave, I can't stay here,'" Rao recalls. "Lots of stands of people saying things, hula-hoopers and tiny little clothes — they had come from Burning Man!

"It took me a while to understand this, but when [Krishna Das] sings he drops an anchor wherever he goes," says Rao, admitting she eventually came around. "The place was packed when he sang, and everyone got something from it. The people who are coming [to Bhakti Fest] are coming to learn. Otherwise you don't have to go to that festival, you can go to Coachella."

Rao has invited me over to her South

Brooklyn apartment for chai, where she recounts the first kirtan she experienced with her grandfather in the village of Bekal, in the South Indian state of Kerala.

"I would just ask him to play whatever songs I learned in school on [his harmonium], and he said, 'I'll show you how to play it, but you have to sing with me.' So he started to play the harmonium, and I didn't know what he was singing. He said, 'I'm going to sing a line and you sing the same thing back.' Kirtan, right?"

Rao recorded her grandfather's songs on a tape recorder, but never did anything with them. The family eventually came to the States, and Rao didn't think about kirtan again for years.

It was 1996 when she met Krishna Das. "I was just pulled in by the chanting," she says. "It took me back to what I felt when I was nine or ten years old with my grandfather.

"[I] first started chanting with KD at Jivamukti in New York City, that's the only place where it was going on," she remembers. "Then he started being invited to other places, and I traveled with him all over the world. Everywhere we go, wherever it is, it's not very different — a sharing, an honoring of what's in our deepest hearts. When we get into a room with each other and are singing, that's the thread on which all the beads of the mala are strung."

Rao remembers becoming transfixed with Krishna Das' version of an old devotional poem called the *Hanuman Chalisa*. "So here I am, I grew up in India, and I had to come all the way here to New York to learn [that] from a Jewish guy from Long Island," she says with a laugh.

Rao memorized the *Chalisa* for a surprise party on Krishna Das' 50th birthday, and the act of devotion came back around. When she returned to Kainchi Dham, she asked her guru, Siddhi Ma, Maharaj-ji's closest devotee, what she could do in service.

"Go and sing, that's your seva,'" Siddhi Ma told her. "'Go and sing *Hanuman Chalisa*.' Thank goodness that we learned it."

Krishna Das is also grateful. "They say that every repetition of one of these words is a seed that gets planted in the stream of our life, of our heart," he says. "Sooner or later those seeds take root and grow, and they grow into a deeper awareness and a deeper joy. And every repetition of the name is a seed."

"You close your practice by offering the merit of your own practice, not only for yourself, but for the benefit of all beings," Rao adds. "So right away, when you're doing your practice, you've already changed your intention. Intention is so much of it, right? Ram Dass said, 'A moment is not in time and not in space. When we dive into that moment, there's Maharaj-ji.' There's presence, there's awareness, there's love. You can put any other word in there that you want."

Hearing these words, I no longer worried if anything was lost when the devotional aspects of practice were moved into the background — or not immediately apparent — at a kirtan. Not all fans of Krishna Das approach kirtan from a place of religious devotion. Similarly, not all visitors to the Bhakti Center's Thursday night kirtans are planning on donning orange dhotis and banging tambourines in Union Square.

The kundalini practitioners who attend workshops in L.A. with White Sun's Gurujas embrace mantra repetition as a science, from a frame of mind intentionally devoid of sacred association, but glean benefits from their practice just the same.

Ultimately, understanding the

historical or cultural authenticity of kirtan is not necessary for it to have value. The most important thing is that taking up a kirtan practice helps people. It can provide a refuge for those moments when thoughts become overpowering and nonsense becomes all-consuming.

"One is always having to process one's own stuff," says Krishna Das. "Again and again you come up against selfish stuff — greed, anger, and fear. All the stuff that we carry around with us. Chanting continually trains us to release whatever it is we're stuck in, without needing to evaluate or judge or even understand intellectually what's going on. It removes us from that flow, just pulls us back like a magnet would pull something toward itself.

"I don't think it's a learning process. I don't think I've ever been able to learn anything," he adds. "But I keep on remembering to put myself in the sun so I get ripe." ∎

View from the audience during a White Sun performance.

Tejas Menon

MUMBAI KADAK

A wave of singer-songwriters is rising in India

by Jody Amable

THERE'S A HINDI WORD USED often by young people in Mumbai: *kadak*. "It's used to define your chai, or your tea — if the chai is strong, then we say it's kadak," explains Tejas Menon, a songwriter who goes simply by Tejas. While Menon acknowledges the word's typical use, he explains that "kadak" has become a word he and his friends also apply to art and music. (The closest English translation is "pop.")

Menon began his adult life working for an advertising agency, though he more or less moved on from that field a few years ago. He has since devoted himself to India's vibrant independent music scene. He started pursuing music alone, with only an acoustic guitar, and has become a revered pop musician on the Indian subcontinent, thanks in large part to a glut of contemporaries. Indeed, though Indian music has spun its wheels in Bollywood soundtracks for decades, a recent explosion of singer-songwriters is moving the subcontinent's popular music forward.

The new Indian indie music movement has sprung from the same cultural seed that birthed American folk, and contains some music that bears a striking resemblance to classic Americana. Though it has more recently branched out to garage bands and indie DJs, the movement is largely powered by the acoustic guitar and sung in English as a nod to its influences.

"[I] grew up listening to American, Celtic, [and] Irish traditional music on the radio, and the influx of cheap pirated tapes from Southeast Asia," says Bipul Chettri, a guitarist who's currently based in New Delhi. "Most of us also attended schools usually run by Irish nuns and Swiss or German priests and missionaries. We were listening to the likes of Woody Guthrie, Bob Dylan, Pete Seeger, Lead Belly, Robert Johnson, [and] Willie

Parekh & Singh

> "[Film music] is a juggernaut. It's a world of its own, which we are quite far from, though things have begun intersecting occasionally. ... There's definitely more people listening to the non-film music spectrum now than ever before. We're hoping this leads to more live music."
>
> Jivraj Singh

Dixon, apart from the usual pop genres, as all our music teachers in school influenced us to listen to them."

India has long been passed over as a producer of viable commercial music for the rest of the world, though its youth have always consumed the rest of the world's pop — and even some underground — music. Now, India might finally be primed for its own music moment.

Breaking Through

For audiences outside of the subcontinent, the most visible participants in India's singer-songwriter scene are Parekh & Singh, who have been performing together since 2013. "A mutual friend introduced us at his birthday party and asked Nischay [Parekh] to sing me one of his songs," says Jivraj Singh. "After a few well-meaning but directionless shows, we took a year off to do our own thing."

The pair eventually got back in contact, though, and decided not to fight fate. Singh adds, "The friendship that formed made it clear that we were ready to actually begin constructing a shared world of music."

Parekh & Singh are gentle in their approach, pulling on that lovelorn thread that connects decades of singer-songwriters. Their most notable single, "I Love You Baby, I Love You Doll," garnered global press last summer, nabbing them spots in major Western publications like *USA Today*, *Billboard*, and *The Guardian*. The tune is one of nine dreamy, guitar-based songs on their debut full-length, *Ocean*, which the pair released late in 2016.

Rarely seen without their coordinated pastel suits (made exclusively by Barkat Ali & Bros. in Kolkata, established 1910), Parekh & Singh not only create music, but also make highly produced videos full of muted colors and natural light. The understated, appealing video for "I Love You Baby," for example, immediately drew Wes Anderson comparisons in the press.

Still, it's hard to say why Parekh & Singh are the ones to cross over to international renown, since "The Scene," as it's known in India, has been brewing for a good half-decade. Many track its rise to Pune — a city famous for its abundance of universities and other institutions of higher learning. There, students began experimenting artistically with Western styles during the early 2000s. This culminated with the launch of a festival called the NH7 Weekender, aimed at fans of this Western-influenced singer-songwriter music, in 2010, and India's

first new genre in decades was born. "[A festival] was unheard of [at the time]," says Menon, adding, "It became such a big movement in the last five to six years."

Menon was a student in Pune when he started writing songs. He never wanted to go to college. "I always told my parents I wanted to write for a bit, take some time off," he recalls. "It was not received excellently."

While working on an economics degree, he got an internship at a radio station, eventually snagging a late-night slot on air. After his shift, he'd use the empty studio to write songs on a guitar and record his work. He started uploading his late-night noodlings to his SoundCloud account, and fans found their way there. "I used to just play a little bit for my friends, and finally when this festival happened, I was like, 'I could probably do this [for a living].' "

Though Menon has since moved on to a much more radio-friendly sound — he makes no secret about pop music being his true love — he maintains a singer-songwriter's spirit.

In 2014 he and his friend Krish Makhija created Kadak Apple Records, a collective for independent musicians in India, many of them singer-songwriters. Kadak Apple makes sure its artists get

polished videos, high-res photos, and slick PR packages, all of which are a natural part of an indie artist's arsenal in the States, but India's independent music scene is still so young that even obtaining professional photos can be a bit of an afterthought for artists and bookers.

"[Venues] would just say, 'Yeah, send me something about the artist,'" Menon explains. "They wouldn't say, 'Send me an electronic press kit, send me high-res images.' We found out it's super-unstructured here … we need to form this kind of collective to do a few things, really small things that make a difference." He's hoping Kadak Apple's treatment of artists will help legitimize and galvanize the scene he's sort of helped found, and maybe — finally — put all eyes on India.

"I really do want to see a cultural export," he says. "I mean, there are a bunch of crossover artists [from elsewhere] in the world. There's the Scorpions [from Germany] or Shakira [from Colombia] … why is it taking so long for there to be somebody from India?"

Of course, the list of Indian artists to make even a blip on America's musical radar is short: It pretty much stops with Ravi Shankar. Currently, the closest analog is Swet Shop Boys, the Indian-American/Pakistani-British duo producing scathing hip-hop that eviscerates the prejudice faced by many Indians abroad. But Swet Shop Boys are not folk, and they're not actually from India.

Beyond Bollywood

For years, popular music in India revolved around Bollywood — an industry that generated $4.5 billion in 2016. Bollywood has had an incredible influence on culture the world over, but it has created a largely impenetrable blockade that impedes other Indian music genres from gaining much traction. Until now.

"[Film music] is a juggernaut," asserts Singh. "It's a world of its own, which we are quite far from, though things have begun intersecting occasionally. … There's definitely more people listening to the non-film music spectrum now than ever before. We're hoping this leads to more live music."

Because of the reach of Bollywood, much of the subcontinent's music industry is closely tied to film, but artists like Tejas Menon have found ways to harness that influence. Menon readily admits he is not so much a movie buff as he is a comic book reader, but he wields the art of storytelling in his work — he's written songs set in and inspired by space, directly related to his love of science and science fiction. Still, his first big single blew up when it was used in a film soundtrack. "That was the first thing I could tell my parents without, like, flinching," he says.

In addition to Bollywood's dominance, the influence of American film can be felt in India's independent music scene. Parekh & Singh make no secret of their love for American film. In addition to their Wes Anderson-esque music videos, their 2016 release *Ocean* folds in clear American cinematic influences — most notably when a bit of dialogue from Woody Allen's *Annie Hall* floats by in "Hill."

"We are boisterous fans of the movies," admits Singh. "Nischay's favorite film is *The Terminal*, and mine is *Star Wars: A New Hope.*" They're not alone. Kadak Apple artist Short Round — real name Jishnu Guha — culled his stage name from the plucky sidekick in *Indiana Jones and the Temple of Doom.* Of course, with its booming population, India makes up the second-largest geographic market for film in the world, behind China and in front of the United States.

Even removed from the heavy American film influence, Indian indie music also just sounds, well, very American. Right down to the fact that some people call it "folk" — even though actual Indian folk music tends to take on a different compositional structure and is played on different instruments.

"There is a difference when you talk about folk music in our part of the world," says Bipul Chettri. "India … has over 22 major languages and over 1,500 dialects spoken in various parts of the

Bipul Chettri

country. So each state and sometimes even districts have their own form of music and lyrics, which may sound totally different from the next one. But the basic tenet of the folk medium remains the same."

On Chettri's early work, like 2014's *Sketches of Darjeeling*, the whines of some background instrumentation sound nearly identical to the straining strings of old plains songs of the American West, and album opener "Mountain High," retains a jangling stomp that is textbook blues. "Allarey Jovan," off Chettri's most recent record, *Maya*, sounds like bluegrass in places.

Chettri is ethnically Nepali, but was raised in India, the son of a Gurkha soldier. "[My father was] also a serious musician and had a band of his own ... music was a part of family life."

Chettri uploaded the guitar-driven "Wildfire" to SoundCloud on a whim. After it gathered steam on the internet, he decided to write a few more songs, and

eventually had enough for an album. "The music I started writing and composing has taken a sound which, I think, sits comfortably in any kind of space, in any part of the world. The nuances of folk, blues, jazz, and rock music are ingrained in [my songs]."

Like so many musicians around the world, Chettri as a child studied classical guitar, which eventually led him to pursue the freer traditions of folk. "Classical guitar perhaps indirectly helped me realize the need for intuitional space in music," he says. "Somehow, while playing classical music, I felt a little incomplete. When I started playing the kind of music I was composing, I could immediately feel a sense of what I was missing all the while."

But even with several years of buzz behind India's indie singer-songwriter scene, not everyone's on board with how many artists have joined the scene. Many artists report having a hard time finding places to play. To many Indians outside

the scene, acoustic music is still thought of as a fleeting trend, something made for and by young people who aren't serious about music.

"We were always programmed as, like, the opening act," Menon laments. "I always found that strange, because some of the biggest names in the world are just [solo artists], like Adele, Taylor Swift, Ed Sheeran."

With so many talented artists stepping up on the subcontinent, though, venues are going to have to start accommodating them soon. In the seven years since it launched, the NH7 Weekender has expanded to eight cities, and *Rolling Stone India* recently came calling for Kadak Apple artist Mali. Parekh & Singh just recorded their first BBC session. And more eyes and ears are turning their way.

"A lot of people are making music, but the number of active venues is at an all-time low," laments Singh. "Fortunately, the only way forward is up." ∎

Yirrmal

SUNRISE TO SUNSET

Yirrmal leads a new generation of indigenous Australian music

by Samuel J. Fell

> **"The manikay, the songline, is in me already. [My people] sing from deep down, to the earth. That was my first tradition."**
> Yirrmal

HIS VOICE IS PURE. HIGH and strong, it thrums like taut wire, resonating with a power that belies his young age. At 22, Yirrmal Marika shows signs of a talent set to bloom — a talent that could one day see him placed alongside his mentor Archie Roach, or other seminal artists like Ruby Hunter, Geoffrey Gurrumul Yunupingu, and Yothu Yindi, whose work has come to define an important part of Australian contemporary music and shines a light on often dark parts of Australia's past.

"He's an amazing young musician," muses Roach. "When I hear Yirrmal sing live ... it cuts right through you, it's just so powerful."

Last November, Yirrmal released his debut cut, an EP titled *Youngblood*. In commercial music terms, it's essentially a folk album: Largely acoustic, it features storytelling set to a simple sound, with an emphasis on the lyrical content as opposed to the instrumentation. It showcases the young man's emerging songwriting talent, his skill on the guitar, his passion for what he's doing. It's not a

release that'll shake the music world to its core, but *Youngblood* offers a glimpse of what the Australian roots music scene can expect in the years to come. It is a foundation from which Yirrmal will no doubt build as he comes to terms with his talent, solidifies his vision, and immerses himself further into his ancient heritage and its culture and philosophies.

Yirrmal is a Yolngu man, an indigenous Australian. Hailing from Yirrkala, in northeast Arnhem Land on the northern edge of the country — locals call it the Top End — his people have one of the oldest cultures on the planet. It's from this ancient tradition that Yirrmal draws inspiration. It informs his music; it's the fertile earth in which his very being is rooted.

Yet, despite the fact he sings mainly in the Yolngu language — putting to song the stories of time and creation passed down from one generation to the next by his people — he sets his stories to Western folk music. This is where his sound intersects with that of his mentor. Roach, a man of both Gunditjmara and Bundjalung heritage — and one of the most respected musicians in Australia, indigenous or otherwise — is also largely a folk player, and has been since his debut release, *Charcoal Lane*, back in 1990.

While Yirrmal and Roach are touchstone artists, they're also just two of many indigenous Australians who

Archie Roach

have combined their storytelling traditions with a Western musical form, whether it be folk, country, blues, soul, gospel, rock and roll, or hip-hop. Indeed, indigenous musicians utilizing Western music has become such a part of the Australian music world since it became mainstream here in the early 1990s that it's no longer regarded as odd, surprising, or a genre of its own merely because its purveyors are of a different race. Indigenous culture, after all, is built on the tradition of passing down stories and legends, so this tradition translates well to Western songwriting styles.

"It's just progression," reasons Roach. "Yirrmal especially. His music surrounds a lot of his stories and culture. For years, we've been doing it — it's just an aspect of storytelling or communicating. [Adding] Western instruments, like guitars, keyboards ... is just a continuation of that old culture [of] communicating and educating."

Heart Beating Harder

Yirrmal grew up around Western-influenced music. His father is the widely respected artist Witiyana Marika — a singer and dancer in seminal indigenous group Yothu Yindi (Yolngu for "Child-Mother"), which played a pivotal role in introducing elements of the music and culture of aboriginal Australia to a mainstream audience in the 1990s. Set to a contemporary rock sound enhanced by traditional instrumentation — yidaki (didgeridoo) and bilma (ironwood clapsticks) — Yothu Yindi achieved worldwide success. In the process, they opened the door for a slew of other indigenous artists who had already been melding their own storytelling traditions with Western contemporary music for decades.

"My biggest idol is Yothu Yindi," Yirrmal says. "Watching them is ... my real inspiration. They pushed me to Western music, and every time their sound comes out, my heart [beats harder]. When I was younger, my heartbeat and my spirit [said], I want to be on that stage someday. And I didn't stop dreaming that.

"The sound of [Yothu Yindi] is so beautiful," he adds. "It just goes into my veins. ... The manikay, the songline, is in me already. [My people] sing from deep down, to the earth. That was my first tradition. We have our own tune that we sing ... and [when] it's combined with the [Western] music, that's my passion."

In 2000, Australian writer Clinton Walker released his highly regarded book *Buried Country*, which recounts the history of aboriginal country music, going back to the 1940s. In an essay describing how he came to write the book, Walker notes, "I was able to discern the aboriginal tradition that existed in country music. ... It wasn't just white artists ripping off black music, or black artists sneaking into the mainstream (predominantly white) charts. It showed me that black and white music was a constant churn of miscegenation."

"It's easy to say that rock and roll ripped off black music, that it ripped off blues and R&B," Walker says today. "But I think you've gotta go further back and say, I don't think the blues would have come about in the antebellum Deep South had the slaves there not been exposed, influenced by, and taken in the influence of, say, Celtic folk music, had they not picked up guitars, which had come from Spain.

"If you go way back, what happened in the cultural melting pot of the Deep South at that time was [that] the black slaves would not have invented some of the new forms they invented, had they not ripped off things from the white fella. I'm completely unashamed in proclaiming that. So therefore, I wasn't so freaked out that the Rolling Stones would cover blues songs, and I wasn't freaked out so much — and a lot of people were completely freaked out — [about] why would an aboriginal person sing a redneck hillbilly white fella country song? Well, we've all been swapping all this stuff all along anyway. It's all just part of the ongoing churn."

This, then, is essentially Australian roots music, stemming from the country's indigenous people, channeled through a modern form.

Melbourne, in the country's south, is a hotbed for what most would regard as Americana or alternative country. But go further beneath the surface, start looking for the music that is native to this country, and you find it with indigenous people, intertwined with all manner of styles: Dan Sultan is a renowned young purveyor of soul and rock and roll; A.B. Original's powerful message is funneled through hip-hop; Geoffrey Gurrumul Yunupingu has touched on folk, soul, and gospel music via his three solo albums; Kev Carmody, Gawurra, Yirrmal, Thelma Plum, Archie Roach, and Ruby Hunter are all folkies; Jessica Mauboy is a pop star;

Jimmy Little, Vic Simms, and Roger Knox all are fine country artists of their respective times. They are but a few indigenous Australian artists who are part of the churn, as Walker calls it.

Next to many of them, Yirrmal is only at the start of his journey, but he is carrying a lot. His songs, the stories they contain, are the lifeblood of Yirrmal's people. They've been passed from generation to generation and it's these songlines — manikay, as they're called by the Yolngu people — that truly inform Yirrmal's, and many other indigenous musicians', work.

"He does carry those songlines within him," says Roach, who provided backing vocals on a couple of the tracks on *Youngblood.* "He grew up with those

Gurrmul

songlines, and he communicates them so effectively through music, through Western music, like Gurrumul's been doing for a while. Yirrmal is a young person who's quite a force."

Finding Identity

Geoffrey Gurrumul Yunupingu is perhaps the indigenous Australian artist best known to international audiences. A featured player with Yothu Yindi in the 1990s, Gurrumul released his eponymous solo debut in 2008 to widespread acclaim. He followed it up in 2011 with *Rrakala*, which did equally well, landing him tour dates in the United States, where he performed for President Obama, as well as in the UK and Europe. *Rolling Stone* called him "Australia's Most Important Voice," and with good reason.

Gurrumul, who's been blind since birth, doesn't speak to the press, at least not directly. Also a Yolngu man, with minimal exposure to the Western world during his youth (aside from the Methodist missionaries who worked on Elcho Island, where he's from), he has no concept of how the media or the music industry works, so is guided by his long-time friend, bassist, manager, and label boss Michael Hohnen. Hohnen runs Skinnyfish Music, based in the Northern Territory capital of Darwin, the closest mainland city to Arnhem Land, and works with a range of indigenous artists.

When talking about Gurrumul, Yirrmal, and indigenous music as a whole, Hohnen uses the word "identity" a lot.

"Cultural identity is everything for a lot of these artists," he says. "You go to France and you sit with French people, there's so much about their joy, which is their identity. And I think Australia is really struggling with how to own their identity. So it's everything to these people up here.

"When you look at Australia as a whole, and talk about identity, I think it's a fantastic topic because, albeit controversial, it's very important," he continues. "Kev [Carmody] and Archie [Roach] and these elder statesmen of aboriginal contemporary music have been singing about the same stuff Briggs [of hip-hop duo A.B. Original] is now bringing up, in a way, but he's more in your face. ... For [A.B. Original] to call [their 2016] album *Reclaim Australia* is enormous — [it's like] holding that up against some white supremacist group and taking their name back."

Melbourne-based indigenous rock and roll/soul artist Dan Sultan echoes that. "I think [indigenous identity] is strong, not just in music but in general," he says. "Identity and pride, I think, is very strong in this country. And I think that just comes out of genocide, you know? If people are marginalized and persecuted ... then we need to be strong, we need to have that steadfast, strong will to just even be here, let alone succeed."

As with many native peoples in nations around the world, indigenous Australians have been maligned over the years by the white majority and their prevailing culture. There was the genocide of which Sultan talks, over the period from settlement until as recently as the 1920s. There was the forced separation of indigenous children from their families in the first half of the 20th century, a group referred to as the Stolen Generation. And there have been countless other events, words, and acts in more contemporary history that have pushed Australia's First Peoples further into the background of our social fabric.

These events also make up a good deal of lyrical content among indigenous artists' work. In 1990, for example, Archie Roach wrote a song about the Stolen Generation titled "Took the Children Away." More recently, the lead single off A.B. Original's *Reclaim Australia* album was titled "Australia Day." It comments on the use of January 26 as Australia's National Day, which eschews the importance of indigenous peoples' history. Jan. 26, 1788, was the approximate date the First Fleet arrived from England, effectively beginning the persecution of the indigenous people. It's a date that is more and more frequently called Invasion Day by a growing number of Australians, black and white.

Of course, while these musicians are heavily aware of their heritage and what it means to be an aboriginal Australian these days, the music they make, regardless of style, is truly core to their being.

"I've always seen myself as a musician first, who just happens to be aboriginal," reasons Sultan. "I think good music is good music. At the end of the day, a musician is a musician, regardless of where they come from, or where their parents are from, or their heritage. I'm very proud of where I'm from, very proud of my heritage. I always have been and always will be."

Then, after a beat, he adds, "I just play rock and roll, man."

Room to Grow

At this early stage, Yirrmal just plays folk. It's likely this will change, though, as the young musician listens more widely, broadening his musical horizons and taking on more influences. It's a natural progression for one who's wanted this almost his entire life.

"I was probably six years old," Yirrmal says of when he realized he wanted to be a musician. "My heart told me that ... if I follow, it [will lead me] to the reality. And it did, you know? I just kept trying, went to school. Stuart Kellaway, the bass player in Yothu Yindi, was the music teacher at school. I just wanted to play the guitar. I was bullied at the school, I was told not to play ... but a good friend took me to his house, gave me his guitar, and he showed me how to play. He said, 'Play A minor,' and he showed me how to play it, and I played that chord for three years."

He laughs, acknowledging how far

he's come since then. He co-wrote *Youngblood* with a couple of prominent musicians — Shane Howard of Goanna and Neil Murray, founder of the mostly-indigenous Warumpi Band. He has big plans. He talks of finishing technical college while working toward his debut long-player and spending a good deal of time on the road. He dreams of playing in front of a crowd of 50,000 people, his music touching them all.

When asked, Yirrmal seems unfazed by the perception that indigenous artists are different from their white counterparts. This is both refreshing and a little worrying. As Sultan noted, "We [indigenous Australians] need to be twice as good to get half as much in anything. That's the way it is — we're kind of starting from behind the eight ball." In order to truly move forward, then, Yirrmal may yet need to confront what is still a barrier for many.

What is fully refreshing though, is his connection with his heritage. "It's very important to me — very important," he says. "It's who I am; [it's] what is aboriginal. And it's home, that connection with the land. The culture is very important, very strong. Culture can make you do something — it's giving me power, pushing me to something."

Yirrmal's father, Witiyana, is strong on culture, prominent among the Yolngu people. It's from his father, as well as the rest of his family, that Yirrmal takes his inspiration.

"[Family] is very important," he explains, talking of how humble his grandfather was, how strong a leader he was. He talks of the education he received as a young Yolngu man, the passing on of the stories of creation, rights, and how to be a man. All of this colors Yirrmal's music, but also his life as an indigenous Australian, which many see as an important aspect, particularly for someone with a platform.

"We've sat down and talked," says Roach, "and I've just told him how important not just his music, but he is, as a young indigenous fella — a First Nation fella, an example for younger people."

Yirrmal is aware of the leadership role he's expected to play among his people as he grows older, but while it is very important to him, it's something for the future. "I'm putting the leadership thing to one side. I don't want to worry about that yet," he explains. "I want to focus on my music. That's my passion. I'm just going to keep going on, playing music, share my heart where people are, and tell my stories about my country, about all Arnhem Land and how its history began — from sunrise to sunset."

Just as important as being a leader — and indeed, part of being a leader — is Yirrmal's determination to share his heritage, and the experience of being an indigenous person, through his music, with the rest of Australia.

"I would love, as a Yolngu leader, to set an example ... [as to] what it means to be an aboriginal person in this country, [especially] a young aboriginal person."

Yirrmal isn't seeking to fix what society has broken over the past two centuries or so. The systemic oppression of race, while lessening with time, still exists. The best Yirrmal can do is to be the best version of himself — as a young indigenous man, a young person, a young musician, no matter the musical style he's utilizing to get his message across. To this end, he's already well on his way.

"I think he'll be one of the major, must-see people," says Roach, looking toward the future. "As a musician, as a person, he's gonna be a force to reckoned with. I can't wait to see what else he does." ∎

"Identity and pride, I think, is very strong in this country. And I think that just comes out of genocide, you know? If people are marginalized and persecuted ... then we need to be strong, we need to have that steadfast, strong will to just even be here, let alone succeed."

Dan Sultan

HILLY-BILLY MUSIC

50 years ago, Bluegrass 45 helped stringband music take root in Japan

by Denis Gainty

O N A WARM AUGUST NIGHT in 2016, high in the mountains above Kobe, Japan, the Takarazuka Bluegrass Festival swung into gear. More than five hundred bluegrass enthusiasts from Japan and beyond had gathered on the steep hillside campground for the festival's 45th consecutive year, making it the third longest-running bluegrass festival in the world. Since 1972, the brothers Watanabe Toshio and Inoue Saburo have put on the festival, modeled after their own experiences as young men in the United States.

As at most Japanese festivals, the audience paid only sporadic attention to the main stage, preferring for the most part to mill around from campsite to cabin, connecting with old friends and picking tunes in jam circles. But as dusk fell on the festival's final evening, those assembled put aside their own music for a chance to celebrate a special milestone in the bluegrass world. With their band mates Lee Chien-Hua, Liao Hsueh-Chieng, Otsuka Akira, and Otsuka Tsuyoshi, Toshio and Sab took the stage as Bluegrass 45. Together with the community of fans they'd helped to create over the course of a half-century, Bluegrass 45 launched one more time into a joyful, high-energy celebration of the music they've spread around the world, and which they've made their own.

Bluegrass and Counterculture

In some ways, the story of Bluegrass 45 and its founding is deeply familiar to a particular generation of bluegrassers in the United States, where a growing disenchantment with commercialism and progressive politics led 1960s college students to embrace the simplicity, purity, and authenticity of Appalachian string music. Like in the United States, the 1960s in Japan was a time of countercultural turmoil; emerging from the fear and

deprivation of wartime — and the shock, dislocation, and confusion of the American occupation that lasted until 1952 — Japanese economy and society had begun to find new prosperity and hope. Under the profound influence of Gen. Douglas MacArthur, the Japanese government was reconfigured as a peaceful democracy, and militarism was formally renounced in the Japanese constitution.

But as the United States entered into military conflicts in East and Southeast Asia — first the Korean War, and then Vietnam — the Japanese populace keenly felt their contradictory responsibilities as America's allies in Asia, on the one hand, and as witnesses to the horrors of modern war on the other. Universities in Japan, like those in the United States,

were host to sometimes violent protests, and students took to the streets in startling numbers. Beginning with opposition to the 1960 security treaty with the United States, which seemed to fly in the face of Japan's post-war pacifism by making it a pawn of US cold war militarism, hundreds of thousands of Japanese protesters engaged in sometimes violent clashes with police. In June 1970, a protest against the renewal of the same treaty had over 700,000 participants, with a staggering estimate of 18 million Japanese protesting the Vietnam War from 1967 to 1970. Seeing those numbers, it's hard not to think of our own experience with the '60s, with campus occupations, with Kent State.

In this context, American folk music began to gain popularity in Japan.

Appalachian string music had already entered — referred to in catalogs as "hilly-billy" or "mountain" music before World War II, but generally lumped together with other popular foreign music as "jazz" — and it had flourished during the American Occupation, thanks to Allied radio programming, American films, and the chance for Japanese musicians to play for American servicemen.

Early bands like the Wagon Masters, the East Mountain Boys, and others formed, and entrepreneurial promoters and music publishers like the Tainaka Brothers in Tokyo began to capitalize on the popularity of American string music. But in the turbulent 1960s, Japanese musicians and audiences began to embrace the explicitly political nature of

"Bluegrass 45 was entertaining drunken sailors and navy cadets and foreign tourists. ... We played their requests even when we didn't know the lyrics — or the chords!"

Otsuka Akira

American folk music. Like its American cousin, Japanese bluegrass was a complex community — and it likewise included a number of passionate young musicians who drew on their love of Bill Monroe's music to give voice to their own concerns for their community and their world.

The Making of Bluegrass 45

When Bluegrass 45 formed in 1967 in the busy port city of Kobe, at the Lost City Coffee House — modeled after the hip coffee houses the original Taiwanese owner, Guo Guang-sheng, had encountered in New York City in the early '60s — the city hosted a vibrant mix of people from around the world. Japanese students and professionals rubbed elbows with businessmen, sailors, and tourists from around Asia and beyond, and anti-war activists came face to face with American servicemen on rest and recuperation from Vietnam.

The members of Bluegrass 45 — banjoist Inoue Saburo, bassist Watanabe Toshio, guitarist Lee Chien-Hua, fiddler Liao Hsueh-Chieng, mandolinist Otsuka Akira, and guitarist and lead singer Otsuka Tsuyoshi (Josh) — came together as teenagers. Along with a dozen or so other young bluegrassers, the future members of 45 were hanging around Lost City when the banjo-playing manager, Nozaki Kenji, decided to go on an extended tour of the United States. He turned to Watanabe and other local students to help keep the coffee house

going until he returned, and six of them stepped up to become the house band.

Their experience was radically different from that of most Japanese musicians. As Otsuka Akira puts it, "Back in the '60s and '70s, most of the bluegrass bands in Japan existed as music clubs in colleges. They practiced ten songs, over and over, so they were tight and well-rehearsed. Bluegrass 45 was entertaining drunken sailors and navy cadets and foreign tourists. ... Tight arrangements didn't mean anything to this crowd. We played their requests even when we didn't know the lyrics — or the chords!"

The composition of the band reflected Kobe's combination of traditional and modern, Japanese and worldly. Sab's older brother Toshio, born in 1946 — the same year Bill Monroe made his first recordings with Lester Flatt and Earl Scruggs — had an early interest not just in bluegrass, but in old-time music as well. He had read a booklet put out by Folkways Records and had experienced bluegrass and old-time music firsthand within the fiercely hierarchical, traditional culture of Japanese university music clubs, in which the elder students would line up new members and bark instrument assignments at them, one by one: "Mandolin! Banjo! Banjo! Guitar! Fiddle! Mandolin!"

Seeing an opportunity for music close to home, Toshio replicated the model by assigning his brother Sab the guitar. But when Sab snuck a listen to a tape of Lester Flatt and Earl Scruggs that Toshio had

brought home, his life changed. He still remembers looking out his window at the gentle green waves of rice fields, the kind you find tucked between buildings even in densely populated Japanese cities, listening to "The Old Home Town," feeling like he'd found his musical soul.

Like Sab and Toshio, the Otsuka brothers found themselves connected to bluegrass through the traditional hierarchies of Japanese families and Japanese universities. The youngest of five children, Akira and his older brother Tsuyoshi were exposed to bluegrass through their brother, Yutaka, who attended Momoyama Gakuin University in the mid-'60s. Yutaka formed the Bluegrass Ramblers, which, in a marker of the popularity of bluegrass in Japan, went on to capture first prize at a prestigious national student music competition, beating out the odds-on favorite, the Waseda University jazz band (the "High Society Orchestra").

Lee Chien-Hua and Liao Hsueh-Chieng were, similarly, products of the Japanese university system. Both lived in the Motomachi section of Kobe. When Lee and Liao met in Momoyama Gakuin University's "light music society" — an early Japanese term for any music outside the classical canon — they were startled to realize their shared Taiwanese heritage, home neighborhood, and love of bluegrass music. Both recall the meeting fondly, as well as their introduction to Sab and his tireless enthusiasm. Over summer vacation in 1967, Liao recalls, Sab lived on the top floor of Lee's building, and drilled Lee and Liao relentlessly in the work of Flatt and Scruggs.

The port city of Kobe is a particularly multicultural Japanese town. At the same time, its diversity is more representative of Japan than one might think. Similarly, Bluegrass 45 reflects the international influences that have shaped Japan since before the 20th century.

Toshio and Sab's father experienced the United States as a businessman in the early 20th century, and developed a strong socialist leaning there. Josh and Akira's father had worked in Shanghai before the war, rubbing elbows with Chinese and Westerners alike, and Akira — born in 1948 — remembers growing up listening to Elvis and Hank Williams, Harry James and Dave Brubeck. (Years later, Akira remembers that Bluegrass 45's version of Brubeck's "Take Five" — a ground-breaking work, and one of the first instances of a 5/4 tune by a bluegrass band anywhere — inspired Sam Bush's response to the band at an early '70s festival: "You guys freak me out, man!")

Further, Lee and Liao both represent, in a way, the imperial realities of prewar East Asia. Though Lee's parents had immigrated to Japan from Taiwan — at the time, a colonial territory of Imperial Japan — Lee was counted as a foreign national, and today holds a Taiwanese passport. Liao, similarly, is a Taiwanese citizen; his father, the son of a traditional Chinese doctor from Guangdong and a mother from Japan's Kumamoto prefecture, chose Taiwanese nationality in defiance of the Communist government of mainland China.

Coming to America

The six — Sab and Toshio, Josh and Akira, Liao and Lee — were all playing at Lost City in 1970 when Charles "Dick" Freeland, the founder of Rebel Records and a central figure in American bluegrass, came to the nearby city of Osaka for business. Invited to Lost City,

Freeland was impressed enough with the group to arrange for a US tour in 1971 and their first American LPs: *Bluegrass 45* and *Caravan*, the latter produced by John Duffey. The group's American debut that June, at Bill Monroe's Bean Blossom Festival, marked what is now regarded as the first international bluegrass festival.

But 45's performance at Bean Blossom should be seen as more than just a transcultural novelty. Along with the debut of John Hartford's *Aereo-Plain* band and an early appearance of the young Sam Bush, Courtney Johnson, and Tony Rice in the Bluegrass Alliance, Bluegrass 45's performance at Bean Blossom in '71 signaled an important shift in the bluegrass world. Further, their performance that same year at Carlton Haney's Camp Springs, North Carolina, festival is captured in the documentary *Bluegrass Country Soul*. In that recording — the first documentary film on bluegrass music — we can see not only the energy and skill of the young Japanese players, but also their sheer joy to partake in the exciting growth and change that was early-'70s bluegrass.

And partake they did. Around their third week in the United States, Freeland got word of a contest in Callaway, Maryland, and called to see if he could book the 45 as a guest band. Although Del McCoury was already signed up to perform, the producers offered the group $200 to appear. Freeland turned that down, and entered the members into the contest instead. Together, Akira remembers, the band's members earned $750 in prize money, with three members taking the top three prizes in the individual banjo competition. "Not bad for 1971," he says.

Liao's strongest memory of the tour is less musical, if more startling: "At Watermelon Park in Berryville, Virginia — or maybe it was Camp Springs, North Carolina — I saw [the] promoter Mr. Carlton Haney chasing Mr. Jimmy Martin with a gun in his hand. I thought, 'Now, I'm in *America*!'"

Back in Japan, the members felt obliged to share their delight at having experienced firsthand the American bluegrass scene — the first Japanese band to do so. Just as they had helped introduce Japanese bluegrass to Americans, so they found themselves sharing recordings, photographs, new songs, advice, and memories of the American scene with young Japanese musicians and fans.

Akira remembers spreading the

bluegrass gospel: "We told people: you can buy or rent a car, rent an apartment, go to this festival, to that festival, what to eat; you'll need a tent, these are today's hot bands; if you go to Bean Blossom, you'll see Lester Flatt, Bill Monroe, Jim and Jesse, but if you go to Carlton Haney's festival, you'll see ... and so on."

Following their US debut, the band's members parted ways as they were pulled in other directions by both music and life.

Josh and Akira returned to the United States for another tour in 1972, during which they enjoyed the surreal experience of playing a live performance before the screening of *Bluegrass Country Soul,* the documentary in which they were featured. When they returned from that trip, Akira and Josh split. In Japan, Josh formed the band Leaves of Grass, and Akira moved to America, where he joined Cliff Waldron's New Shades of Grass.

During their years apart, the band's contributions to the bluegrass world — in Japan and beyond — continued. In 1973, Liao was one of the founders of the first Japanese bluegrass magazine, *June Apple,* which introduced so many young Japanese to the culture of bluegrass and its festivals. Sab followed suit years later, in 1983, by launching *Moonshiner,* which continues today as Japan's longest-running bluegrass publication. Sab and

Toshio founded Red Clay Records in 1971. Through B.O.M. Service, Ltd. ("Bluegrass and Old-Time Music") an enduring mail-order business modeled after David Freeman's County Sales, the brothers continue to ship CDs and other media to members of the Japanese bluegrass community, and the Takarazuka Festival they launched in 1972 has been the polestar of the Japanese bluegrass calendar for longer than Chris Thile has been alive. Jerry Douglas wrote the song "Takarazuka" in its honor (sometimes rendered as "Takarasaka"), and Noam Pikelny is the latest American star to make a guest appearance, in 2016.

Throughout the years, the members of the 45 have continued to play, if not together, at least in the joyfully chaotic free-for-all that is Takarazuka.

Lee remembers fondly a late-night appearance in the early '80s, when, after the scheduled bands had finished, the crowd started chanting, "pu-roresu!"

(pro-wrestle). Sab hastily threw up a makeshift ring, and Lee and the emcee — the brilliant mandolinist Tani Goro — got serious.

The story of Bluegrass 45, then, is not simply a story of bluegrass music in Japan. Akira especially has continued his musical career in the States; since Cliff Waldron's New Shades of Grass, he has played in the DC area virtuoso group Grazz Matazz and appeared on dozens of bluegrass, newgrass, and other recordings, including his 2012 solo album, *First Tear*. In 1973, Sab produced Tony Rice's first album, *Got Me a Martin Guitar*, which was retitled *Guitar* in the United States. Sab, unhappy with the small amount of money he'd been able to offer Tony, gave him the rights for its US release. Toshio was the executive producer of the Grammy-nominated *Memories of John*, a John Hartford tribute album featuring a who's-who of the bluegrass world. And in 1995, both Sab and Toshio

were recognized for their lifelong contributions to the genre by the International Bluegrass Music Association, for which Sab served as secretary of the board of directors from 1995 into the early 2000s.

Saved by Music

In January 1995, the Great Hanshin Earthquake struck Kobe. It was centered on the small island of Awajishima, just a few miles from Kobe. Thousands died, mostly in the city of Kobe itself, and hundreds of thousands of buildings were damaged or destroyed, including the homes of band members. Akira and Josh's mother's house, along with Sab and Toshio's family home in nearby Takarazuka, were destroyed. Toshio rebuilt his house and lives there today; Sab is in an apartment minutes away by foot, with his fiddler wife Yuriko. When the earthquake hit, both Liao and Lee

This year, Bluegrass 45 will return to the United States. ... The members will see old friends and reach new American audiences, and show us yet again that bluegrass is bigger than the blinkered nationalism that has stained so much of the last hundred-plus years.

were living in Kobe, and when Lee's apartment was damaged he and his family moved in with Liao.

"After the terrible earthquake, I felt like we were saved by music and friends," says Lee. "The event was so huge, you know." The tragedy marked a turning point not only for Japan, where it is widely remembered for the unprecedented community-based voluntarism that it inspired, but also for the members of Bluegrass 45, who reunited shortly thereafter for a US tour, a live album, and a documentary film.

Last year, at the 45th Takarazuka Festival, the members of Bluegrass 45 demonstrated again their talent, energy, and pure, wild joy. The audience — some five or six hundred Japanese and a handful of foreigners, including a hot young Korean band, an American film crew, Noam Pikelny, and me — were brought into a magic bluegrass celebration of endurance and renewal. In some ways, this is illusory. Like Bluegrass 45, and like the Japanese population itself, the skinny young guys (and, though less often, gals) who fostered such love for Bill Monroe's music in Japan now find themselves mysteriously aged. Liao joked that, to Americans, the members might still look young; he remembers fondly being carded, again and again, when they tried to buy beer in the United States. "In 1971," he says,

"maybe we looked, like, 13 to you American guys." But despite the energy of young groups like the Bluegrass Police and artists like Sab's mandolinist son, Inoue Taro, despite a recent uptick in membership in university bluegrass clubs, and despite the work of brilliant young luthiers like Suda Hiroshi, Japanese bluegrassers find themselves in a near-crisis.

Festival promoters and club owners are aging, and few of the younger generation of musicians are stepping up to take their place in the Japanese bluegrass infrastructure. Asked about the future of bluegrass in Japan, Lee says bluntly: "It's hopeless!"

Sab, as one of the few Japanese ever to make a (modest) living at bluegrass, agrees, but adds, "Sometimes I feel Lee pretends to be a nihilist!"

Sab remembers how Lee used his international business contacts to provide a safety net for "a lot of reckless young bluegrassers who wanted to be professional musicians." Exceptions like Toshio and Sab aside, Japanese bluegrass continues to be a labor of love, and its existence continues to depend more on soul than solvency.

For Sab, though, it's never been about the money. This past year, in his sun-filled apartment in Takarazuka, he shared memories of playing for

American sailors and soldiers at Lost City in the 1960s, during the Vietnam War. He told me how the servicemen, in the midst of a horrific, alienating experience far from home, would often cry at hearing Sab and his friends singing familiar melodies. At that point, Sab himself had to stop talking, choked up by the memories of those connections made across politics and language and culture, offering frightened young men in harm's way a chance to feel another human heart.

This year, Bluegrass 45 will return to the United States. Celebrating their 50th anniversary, they will come again to America to share their love for bluegrass music and the bluegrass community. Accompanied by an American documentary film crew, the members will see old friends and reach new American audiences, and show us yet again that bluegrass is bigger than the blinkered nationalism that has stained so much of the last hundred-plus years. Maybe their example will inspire not only Japanese and American musicians, but the larger world, to imagine the possibility that always exists for a serendipitous, joyfully shared humanity. Or maybe, after all, they'll just put on a really good show. Whatever the case, their place in the history of bluegrass, in Japan and in the world, is secure. ∎

Hanggai

ROGUE CULTURE

**Exploring the Chinese underground
with Abigail Washburn and Hanggai**

by Kim Ruehl

ILCHI IS A MAGNETIC MAN. THIS is especially true onstage, where he wears traditional Mongolian dress: often a robe-like outfit, though videos show him decked out in leather or a pair of jeans and some black boots — almost like something you'd see at the Sturgis Motorcycle Rally, but not quite. Perhaps part of the allure is that nothing about this guy or his band, Hanggai, is what it appears to be at first glance.

The band's name is pulled from the ancient Mongolian language, meaning, as Ilchi told CNN in 2009, "an ideal farmland with blue sky, grassland, mountains, rivers, and forests — a heavenly homeland." This deeply rooted reference to an idyllic rural setting, chosen for a band that formed 13 years ago in the booming metropolis of Beijing, pretty much sums up all the ideas and values that Hanggai was formed to espouse.

In the 2005 documentary film, *Beijing*

Bubbles, which focuses on a handful of bands then-prominent in China's underground punk music scene, Ilchi walks through downtown Berlin, examining a traditional-style Mongolian hat before placing it on his head. He occasionally looks at the camera but doesn't say a word. With the German traffic whizzing by and the large city buildings in the background, the very presence of this crew of Mongolian men in traditional garb, juxtaposed with the

> ## "Cultivating audiences who actually want to listen to independent music is a challenge in China, because people aren't used to it. They're used to the government or the local cultural bureau or the central government cultural bureau filling the radiowaves with whatever they want to fill it with."
>
> Abigail Washburn

striking Western modernity of their surroundings, feels innately punk-rock.

Hanggai could certainly be called a punk band. Augmented by electric guitars and bass, hard-hitting Western-style drum beats pound against the speakers in songs like "The Rising Sun," or even the decidedly folkier "Xiger Xiger." Vocalist Hurizha's rhythmic utterances can be the sonic equivalent of fist pumps in the air. And they count Rage Against the Machine as among their musical heroes. But listen more deeply, behind the smoke of the sonic fire they light, and you'll hear the ancient craft of Mongolian throat-singing, the whine of an erhu, the buzz of a bow against a horsehair fiddle, that heavenly homeland for which they named themselves.

These disparate styles have helped make Hanggai's music accessible for Western audiences, and their frequent touring abroad has reinforced their legitimacy back home, where they're viewed as sort of cultural ambassadors.

"If you come from a small town [in the States] ... and you make it in New York, and you come back to your hometown, you're extra special because you made it, you know? The Chinese population has been dealing with that for a long time because China was behind the rest of the world for so long," explains Jon Campbell, author of *Red Rock: The Long Strange March of Chinese Rock and Roll.* "You can be a wildly successful artist and never leave China. Absolutely. You can be a rich

and famous artist and never leave the country. But if you're of the 'underground,' if you're playing music that's not for the stadium, and you're playing the clubs and maybe even theaters, your goal is to join the rest of the pop-rock world, and the apex of that is not in China. The apex of that is in the West. For that community of musicians, particularly, I think Hanggai is definitely the model."

Last year the group traveled to Nashville to record with producer Bob Ezrin, who has worked previously with Pete Seeger, Lou Reed, Phish, and many others. Ilchi called his friends Abigail Washburn and Béla Fleck — whom he met in 2006 when their Sparrow Quartet was touring China — for some background support, adding yet more Western folk cred.

But back in Berlin, in *Beijing Bubbles*, Hanggai's destination was the Kaffee Burger, a trendy club in the Mitte neighborhood in the center of the city. There, as in Nashville, the band was far from home; they definitely didn't fit in. But as the film presses on and they're introduced to the audience, their music makes them the only thing that really matters in that moment. There is, after all, no other band quite like Hanggai — in Berlin or, for that matter, in China.

Outside the Mainstream

Ilchi and his bandmates are an ethnic minority back home, where around 92

percent of Chinese are part of the Han majority and the other seven-or-so percent of the nation's population is made up of an assortment of ethnic minorities. "Five of [the band members] come from Inner Mongolia," explains Jianyin, Hanggai's tour manager for the Asia market. "One of them comes from Shanghai province, [which] is also a Mongol area. There are a lot of Mongol people in there. ... Ilchi is from Beijing, but

Abigail Washburn

his father and mother came from [the] Mongol area. When he was a child they moved to Beijing, but he's still Mongol."

Washburn, who has lived and toured extensively in China and began her adult life intending to be an international lawyer there before the banjo came calling, explains further. "Hanggai … come from a different culture" than the Han people, she says. "They think differently. They're more of a rogue culture, honestly.

And they're more of a sacrilegious culture. The Mongolians are different than the Han people, there is no doubt about it. They are used to having these tribes of people playing music and traveling around. I think a lot of [Mongolian people] have settled down, but still there are a lot of nomadic people living in Mongolia and that's their nature throughout history. Their genetic code has probably evolved to believe in being a

nomadic people. They're really … a special group of ethnic people living in a Han society."

She adds that the band has done "an amazing job of being independent, rogue musicians while fitting into what the Chinese culture and government needs them to be in order to accept them. It's very, very rare to run into something like that. And I think what makes it sustainable to them is that they have success outside of China."

Sure, in a time when we can all experience the music of any nation through a simple Google search, Hanggai's international audience may not seem particularly remarkable at first glance. But as mentioned, everything about this group goes a little deeper than that.

After all, rock music is not exactly the mainstream music of China. But the fact that Hanggai has found a way to seamlessly pull together their rock-and-roll influences and their deep Mongol roots has given Western audiences an entrance point to their far-flung, little-known-in-the-West tradition. Hang on the Box, meanwhile — one of the other bands featured in *Beijing Bubbles* — is an energetic, gifted, straight-up post-punk band who would make good sense on a festival lineup with Sleater-Kinney and Sonic Youth. Though they pull off the American-style post-punk thing quite well, and are no doubt radical in the context of China's state-run music industry, there's nothing in their music that Western audiences can't also get just as readily from a band in Minneapolis or L.A.

What's more, Mongolian music typically uses a pentatonic scale, which means that it's based on five notes, whereas the diatonic scale typical of Western music contains seven notes. Thus, there can be a slight sonic disconnect between Mongolian folk music and Western ears — the melodic equivalent of speaking in a thick accent. For a person raised on American music, tuning into Mongolian melodies requires at least a little bit of an exercise

in letting go. This is to account for the sort of fetishized exoticism that tends to surround so much of what gets called "world music" by Western audiences. But, just like talking to your new friend from Beijing, once your ears become attuned to their particular inflection when they speak English — or once they become accustomed to yours when you attempt Mandarin — it can feel as though the window you always squinted to look through has incrementally been wiped clear.

Of course, your average listener doesn't know or care about the difference between a diatonic scale and a pentatonic scale, so what matters for a Mongolian group hoping to appeal to Western audiences is whether there's something in the music they can relate to. For Hanggai, this comes through via the electric guitar — or, ever since they met Washburn and her instrument in 2006 — the banjo. It's the spoonful of sugar that helps the medicine (throat singing, for one, and ancient diatonic Mongolian folk melodies, for another) go down.

Another thing Western audiences tend to look for is a unique artistic vision, yet the concept of personal taste and artistic autonomy is a foreign concept to navigate in a nation where relationships and connections between people are valued in the public square much more than individual taste.

"Cultivating audiences who actually want to listen to independent music is a challenge in China," explains Washburn, "because people aren't used to it. They're used to the government or the local cultural bureau or the central government cultural bureau filling the radio waves

with whatever they want to fill it with. They're used to being fed the music they're supposed to be listening to. ... This whole concept of modern folk music — taking your folk music, like we do in America all the time, and making it into your own voice — that's just not a mainstream thing to do there. Again, it's about serving the system. It's about being a part of [something] ... and this is a piece of who Chinese are as people, as humans, in their nature: They're more concerned about their relationships and connections to the people around them than they are about their individuality. So the idea of cultivating individual taste is very odd in that context."

The Right Guanxi

Indeed, the music the central government chooses to proliferate in China is an important thing to explore. It is because of this fact — and China's millennia-old culture — that "folk music" and "classical music" are the same thing in China, preserved and performed by mostly-Han orchestras of classically trained musicians, playing music that serves the purpose of shining light on what it means to be Chinese. And, because seven percent of the country — ethnic minorities like the Mongolian people, the Uighurs, the Yi, etc. — are part of what makes China unique, their traditional music is also deeply valued and celebrated, and supported and promoted by the Chinese government.

"To get a license to publish an album, you need to get a number from the ministry of culture," explains the author

Campbell. "There are varying degrees of state involvement. [The artist or label] submits lyrics and music to the relevant ministry and they give you a number. But there's also the spectacle of central presentations, which are on television. When you talk about folk music, it's wrapped up with the ethnic nationalities that comprise the population. There's 56 ethnic minorities in China. So the state is very eager to present all the minority groups in mainstream ways: television, radio, major concerts."

"There's something called guanxi in China," Washburn carefully explains, taking the whole cultural exchange lesson a step further. "They capitalize on guanxi. It's relationships. If you have the right guanxi, you can do a lot of things. You have to have the right guanxi and respect the guanxi. You can't just ... get an opportunity and fuck everybody over. You have to behave well and use the opportunities well. Otherwise the people who connected you with the opportunities will 'lose faith,' it's called. It's similar in America, but they really do talk about it in a quantifiable amount in China.

"I think China is very proud to have an export of music that people around the world love," she adds, returning to the topic of Hanggai's success, "as long as they're respectful of the Chinese government and their wishes. The fact that Hanggai can pull off being a heavy rock band ... is really great. Now they have an international label that signed them and a booking agent and a tour manager out of Europe."

Where an American folk band might eventually wander into rock or pop music in order to make a more reliable living, then, the opposite was the case for Ilchi and his bandmates. All of the pieces of their career that Washburn says fell into place may not have come together for Hanggai if they had remained predominantly a punk band, which is where they began.

"In the beginning of the band," says Hanggai tour manager Jianyin, "it was a punk band or a metal band. ... But maybe three or four years later, the creator of this band, also now the leader of the band, Ilchi, said he thought he had to make Mongol folk music because he finds [that] more and more Mongol people forget their folk music. [They] listen to popular music or music from out[side] of China, or music from out[side] of Mongolia. He thinks that's a little problem for Mongolian music, so maybe it is worth it. So he changed the style of the band to Mongolian folk music.

"But," she adds, "it also has some of the rock style."

In that way, the band has come full circle over the past dozen years. They began as a metal or punk band, aping Rage Against the Machine, before Ilchi shifted his focus to preserving his roots for future generations. Then they became a hardcore folk band, finding ways to make their ancient music palatable to audiences of their generation. But on 2014's *Baifang* album and even more so on last year's *Horse of Colors*, the electric guitar is decidedly forward in the mix, with the Mongolian instruments playing more of a support role. The balance is still there, though, and it's clear in listening to their music that, with their skills and reverence for their roots, they could just as easily swing back and forth on this pendulum for the rest of their career — as long as their guanxi is preserved.

East and West

In 2006, Washburn says, "the [US] Embassy [got] in touch and said, 'Hey! We'll pay for you to fly over here and we'll give you a cool tour and you're going to represent America culturally.' So the Sparrow Quartet was created as a result of that being the band that wanted to go with me. Ben Sollee, I had been playing with. Casey Driessen had sat in with Ben and I a few times and had been on the record. He was one of my closest friends, and still is. And Béla and I had just started dating and he had helped produce the record. All three of them were like, 'Let's go to China together!' And then we were like, 'This is a weird band.' But the wonderful thing about going to China is that nobody there is judging me by the same standards as I would experience here in America. Nobody's saying, 'Oh — two banjos, a cello, and a fiddle is a weird band.'"

Indeed, halfway across the world, these four exceptional American folk players were just a taste of raw traditional music from the US, an introduction to what is possible on Western stringed instruments. But getting to the point where the embassy would just get in touch with her and invite her to China was the result of years of Washburn's determination to bridge her two great selves: the one that had set out to be a lawyer in China, and the one that, instead, unexpectedly landed a record deal during one fateful weekend at an International Bluegrass Music Association (IBMA) conference.

"That's when all of that experience of

Ajinai

traveling and hearing all that music started coming into play," she recalls, detailing her explorations of China far beyond Beijing. Years earlier, she rode trains through Uighur and Yi country, hearing the traditional music of China's various ethnic groups without the conscientious ears of a practicing musician. Back then, the music Washburn took in was part of the greater cultural exploration she was taking on, to learn about a part of the world that was so unlike her own. The music came the same way the food and the language and the landscape did, and she took it in and took it seriously. So when, years later, she found herself developing a love affair with the banjo, having never before been a musician, naturally all the musical styles she'd soaked in during her life to that point — from the popular music of her youth to the Chinese music of her 20s and

the American folk music she was just discovering — swirled together in what came out through her instrument.

"All the studying I'd done of Chinese culture and language and poetry" came together, she says. "That's when I really started writing songs in Chinese and started laying the groundwork for potentially someday working with Chinese artists, which I never had fathomed until the point I knew I'd be a musical artist. That's when I really started paying attention to the music industry in China, was 2004. ... I was very sad to not be in China pursuing this other life I'd imagined for myself. So I called ... two of my friends [who] happened to be in foreign bands in China — they were foreigners, Canadians. I called them and said, 'I really want to come over and visit because I miss you all. I'll probably bring my banjo and we can jam.'

"One of my friends said, ... 'I've been booking my band at bars lately and I can just set you up a couple gigs.' I was like, 'Yeah, I'm down.'

"So in 2004 and 2005 I took bands with me. I was a new artist but I'd made friends really fast with a couple of young musicians, like Casey Driessen, Amanda Kowalski [formerly of Della Mae], Tyler Grant, and they all were eager to go with me to China even though they wouldn't make any money. ... And once we were over there, we extended our trips — both in 2004 and 2005 — because the embassy in Beijing and the consulate in Chengdu heard about us coming over and said, 'We'll set up some shows for you at schools and call them cultural exchanges.' So that really started everything. This idea became the template for my involvement in the music industry in China for the next 10 years."

Shanren

Soon after, Washburn's friend Campbell — one of the Canadians she mentioned — introduced her to Ilchi and Hanggai. They jammed together, clicked almost instantly, and forged a relationship that had them sharing bills in China for the next four years. Back on the other side of the world, they even shared a stage at Bonnaroo.

Coming Above Ground

Campbell has worked with Hanggai a number of times — both in China and in Canada — and is hesitant to put his finger on what it is that sets them apart from other Chinese musicians. There's a tendency for casual audiences to home in on their ethnicity as a point of fascination. Indeed, most Americans and Canadians are not particularly well-versed in Mongolian tradition. In a world where we're all indelibly connected, there are few things that strike Westerners as new and untapped, so an ethnic minority from the other side of the world, perhaps, speaks to the Western impulse to explore the unknown.

"It's certainly easier to get a gig for Hanggai at a [Canadian] festival than it is to get a gig for the Gang of Four in China — the greatest post-punk band in the whole country," Campbell notes. "The world music industry has taken to them. That's great for them. I've seen them succeed. ... They just came back from Womad [festival] in Chile. I don't want to say it's because they're ethnic minorities and they're throat singing instead of strumming a guitar. [But] other bands that want to go abroad are having a tougher time of it because they don't have the ethnic tradition."

That said, Campbell goes on to note that, since Hanggai has succeeded outside of China, other minority bands have popped up with an interest in celebrating their ethnic roots as well. For starters, former Hanggai member Hugejitu spun off into a more psychedelic Mongolian folk band called Ajinai, which has toured Canada with Campbell's help and done a number of jaunts through Mexico. Shanren is a group from the Yunnan province in Southwest China, comprised of members from the Wa and Buyi ethnic groups. Built around Chinese stringed instruments like qinqin, Shanren has had some success in Europe and are quite popular back home as well. Manhu is a Yi band headed for their first run of the States this September. And of course, there will be more. Given all this, it is fair to say the Chinese underground is coming up for air. And when it surfaces, it can thank Hanggai for clearing the way. ■

THANK YOU TO THE ARTISTS AND WRITERS WHO HAVE SHARED THEIR PART OF THE WORLD WITH US.

Illustration by Colin Sutherland

she come by it natural

Part Two:

Young Dolly Parton masters the art of leaving

This is the second installment in a four-part series by our No Depression Writing Fellow, Sarah Smarsh. She is spending 2017 writing about Dolly Parton. Read the next installments in the Fall and Winter 2017 issues of this journal.

By Sarah Smarsh

In late 2014, *Billboard* magazine asked Dolly Parton about feminism. "Are you familiar with Sheryl Sandberg's book *Lean In*?" the interviewer inquired.

"What is it?" Parton asked.

"*Lean In* — it is a book," the interviewer explained. "Have you ever 'leaned in'?"

"I've leaned over," Parton said, cracking herself up with a possible innuendo. "I've leaned forward. I don't know what 'leaned in' is."

That an iconic female trailblazer in music, business, and popular culture wasn't up on the feminist conversation du jour reveals where Parton came from: a place where a woman's strength and independence is more about walk than talk. In the women's movement, that talk — the articulation, study, and theories of advancement toward gender parity — has been crucial to social progress. Of equal import and less acclaim, though, is what working-class women like Parton do for the cause.

Their worlds often resist the container of politicized terminology that is often the exclusive province of college-educated people. But working-class women have seen the most devastating outcomes of gender inequality. Impoverished mothers with hungry children, abused wives too poor and rural to access the legal system, work that is not only undervalued and underpaid but makes the fingers bleed. For these women, the fight to merely survive is a declaration of equality that could be called "feminist." But here's the thing: In my experience, right or wrong, they don't give a shit what you call it.

Earlier this year, the Women's March and related strike on International Women's Day again exposed the old class chasm that tends to run through any political movement. With the Oval Office newly occupied by an admitted sexual predator, today's crucial political resistance owes much to the hard work and fury of civically engaged women. Who is able to participate in such activism has a lot to do with economic agency, though. You can bet that most photos of marchers wearing pink "pussy" hats document middle- or upper-class women able to take time away from work, obtain transportation to a protest site, or afford a babysitter.

For a woman like me, a feminist who grew up in a place that was more like Dolly Parton's childhood home in rural Tennessee than like a well-connected progressive hub, marches and strikes are simultaneously something to cheer and look upon with some skepticism. I'm proud to call myself a feminist but feel no self-satisfaction about my framework for what the word means — a privilege of education and culture most women where I'm from have not experienced.

Working-class women might not be fighting for a cause with words, time, and money they don't have, but they possess an unsurpassed wisdom about the way gender works in the world. Take, for example, the concept of intersectionality. The poor white women who raised me don't know that term, but they readily acknowledge that the dark-skinned women they know face harder battles than they do, in many ways. They know this from working on factory floors and in retail stock rooms alongside women of color who they have watched endure both sexism and racism along with their poverty.

There is, then, intellectual knowledge — the stuff of research studies and think pieces — and there is experiential knowing. Both are important, and women from all backgrounds might possess both. But we rarely exalt the knowing, which is the only kind of feminism many working women have.

Leaving Home

Parton's career took off at the same moment the women's liberation movement did, providing a revealing contrast between feminism as political concept and feminism embodied in the world. Like most women in poverty, Parton knew little of the former but excelled at the latter. You won't get very far as a poor woman without believing you are equal to men. The result of that belief is unlikely to be a "leaning in," Sandberg's possibly sound advice to middle- and upper-class women seeking to claim the spoils enjoyed by the men in their offices and homes. A poor woman's better solution is often to turn around and walk away from a hopelessly patriarchal situation that she cannot possibly mend with her limited cultural capital.

First, Parton left Sevier County, Tennessee, where she famously came up slopping hogs and wearing rags as one of 12 children in a two-room cabin. By the time she took off, she had sensed herself a star and been hustling recording opportunities with an uncle's help for years. The moment she finished high school, she got on a Greyhound bus pointed toward Nashville.

It was 1964, a presidential election year, and the country was torn by political uprising and tragedy. Young men were beginning to return from Vietnam in caskets, and President John F. Kennedy had been assassinated less than a year prior.

In her 1994 autobiography, *Dolly: My Life and Other Unfinished Business*, Parton recalled hearing news of Kennedy's death over her boyfriend's car radio while en route to perform on the Cas Walker radio show during a school break.

"I had loved John Kennedy ... in the way one idealist recognizes another and loves him for that place within themselves that they share," she wrote. "I didn't know a lot about politics, but I knew that a lot of things were wrong and unjust and that Kennedy wanted to change them." Her boyfriend, however, had responded to the announcement by calling Kennedy a "nigger-lovin' son of a bitch." She promptly dumped him.

"I couldn't believe that young person with whom I had shared intimacy and laughter could be so ignorant, biased, and insensitive," she recalled.

Congress was on the cusp of passing the Civil Rights Act, but the women's liberation movement of the 1960s and '70s had not yet reached fever pitch. Kennedy had created a commission on the status of women before his death, but the National Organization for Women did not yet exist. Strict, conformist gender roles still trapped females of all socioeconomic classes as wives, mothers, and second-class citizens.

The irony of a song called "Dumb Blonde" — an admonishment of a man who calls a woman stupid — being Parton's big break is rich. Its theme of a woman being smarter than the man who underestimates her would be a recurring one throughout her career.

When Parton stepped off the bus in Nashville, the most transformative feminist texts of that movement were yet to be published, but they likely wouldn't have reached Parton anyhow. The women of her area were too busy feeding hungry mouths, too isolated from discourse in a pre-internet, rural place, to read such literature — written in a form of English they didn't speak, anyway. That Parton even learned to read was a privilege that her father, a farmer and sometimes coal miner who was illiterate for lack of schooling, didn't share. But Parton was living feminism without reading about it. Leaving home alone, as a woman with professional aspirations and no financial means, demonstrated that she wanted a better life and thought she deserved it, though no model existed for the journey ahead beyond her own imagination.

Meanwhile, the place where she'd pursue that life — the recording capital of country music — couldn't have been a more harrowing gantlet for a woman. Even if America had by then put a few small cracks in the ceiling that held women down, Nashville was squarely situated under the thickest glass.

Patsy Cline, who died in a plane crash the year before Parton got to town, had recently challenged the industry's old-boy network, in which women almost never headlined shows. In 1960, she dared to wear pants on the Grand Ole Opry and was called over by a male host to be reprimanded before the crowd. That was the sort of heat headstrong Cline was born to take and dish back, but she couldn't beat economic injustice as she trail-blazed for her gender. According to the PBS documentary *American Masters: Patsy Cline*, her first record deal, in the 1950s, gave her half the industry-standard pay rate men received and reserved all publishing rights for her label. This enslaved her voice to the studio's demands. But Cline — eager to escape her own poor, working-class origins in Virginia — found it preferable to her previous job slitting chicken throats on an assembly line.

It was a hard row for a female singer-songwriter, and Parton's dreams didn't materialize as quickly as she'd hoped. She was soon so broke she fed herself by stealing food from grocery stores or roaming hotel hallways in search of room-service trays left outside doors for pickup.

Over the course of a few years, she made a small name for herself around town doing mercenary gigs: live spots on early-morning radio shows, a jukebox convention in Chicago. She garnered attention as the uncredited backup singer on a hit pop song she had co-written with her uncle, "Put It Off Until Tomorrow," which was named BMI Song of the Year. The next year, 1967, Parton finally got the chance to cut her first country song, "Dumb Blonde." It became a top-10 hit.

The irony of a song called "Dumb Blonde" — an admonishment of a man who calls a woman stupid — being Parton's big break is rich. Its theme of a woman being smarter than the man who underestimates her would be a recurring one throughout her career. Parton didn't write that song, as she would most of her hits to come, but she lived it so thoroughly that she couldn't even perform it on television without a man doing the precise thing the song articulates.

To perform her popular number on the syndicated *The Bobby Lord Show*, 21-year-old Parton wore a fitted orange dress with a high neckline. Her massive blond beehive may have reached a couple inches higher than the mainstream norm, but there was no obvious trace of country or the over-the-top look for which she's now known.

When Parton spoke, though, her East Tennessee accent showed, as did the fact that she was more capable than the male host. Someone had written a goofy segue to her performance in which Lord was supposed to cleverly call her a dumb blonde with a well-timed pause — as in, "Why don't you go sing, dumb blonde," rather than, "Why don't you go sing 'Dumb Blonde.'" Parton did her part — act confused and smile — but even on the second try Lord couldn't deliver the line right, and the joke flopped.

Still, suffering those sorts of indignities for exposure or a small check turned out to be a good gamble. Porter Wagoner, whose country music hour was the number-one nationally syndicated show on television, said he'd been following Parton's work and saw "something magical" in her, she recalled in her autobiography. Would she join his show? The salary offer: 60 grand.

It was a rip-off considering Wagoner and the show's wealth, but it was a fortune in Parton's eyes. She said yes, of course.

Parton's big risk — leaving home as a teenager without two dimes to rub together at an age by which her own mother was already married with two children in a Smoky Mountain holler — had paid off. She had ended up in another sort of bind, though: what would turn out to be a long, often torturous tenure alongside the male host's thunderous ego on *The Porter Wagoner Show*. But Parton would never haunt hotel hallways seeking scraps of room-service meals again.

With that first bit of money, according to that 2014 interview with *Billboard*, Parton bought her first new car. She was married by then, to a man who ran a concrete-pouring business, but the new blue station wagon was paid for with her money. Still, his preferences decided what kind of car it would be.

"I think it was a Chevrolet," Parton said, "because Carl, at that time, only drove Chevrolets."

Like many women at the time and certainly poor ones, she didn't know how to drive. En route to record with Wagoner for the first time, she drove the car into the wall of Nashville's Studio A. That she rolled up and knocked bricks off a powerful recording studio in the man's world where she was tearing down walls has some poetic significance. The bricks were replaced but never quite matched.

"When [the studio] used to do tours," she told *Billboard*, "they'd go around and say, 'This is where Dolly Parton ran into the wall.'"

Having Enough

Most poor women's risks don't pay off with fame and fortune. But the lives of the women I grew up around — airplane-factory workers, cafeteria cooks, discount-store cashiers, diner waitresses, office assistants, fast-food workers — all contain a common thread of dramatic, self-preserving departures. The stories they told me about their pasts and presents could be boiled down to a recurring line: "I had enough of his shit."

The "he" in the story might be an abusive husband, a cheating boyfriend, a sexist boss. Sometimes it was a place rather than a man that was hostile toward a woman — the small Colorado town that ostracized my then-20-something grandmother for wearing mini-skirts and not behaving "properly" in the 1960s or the Virginia military base where my aunt was shamed for being pregnant out of wedlock. For them, the act of leaving wasn't so much hopeful as it was necessary for survival, whether physically or psychologically. Often, my family's circumstances and likelihoods being what they were, the next man or place was no better the last. But they could leave again, and they did. By the time she was 32, my grandma Betty had divorced six men.

The first one shot her. The second one kidnapped her son. The third one broke her jaw. The fourth one was a brief business arrangement: She could show the courts she had a husband, as an attorney had insisted amid her attempts to get her son back, and he, a Mexican immigrant, could get his US visa. The fifth turned out to be irrevocably emotionally scarred from his time serving in Vietnam. The sixth one was verbally critical of Betty and my mom, who by then was a teenager.

As my grandma would say about any untenable situation she left behind, "It wasn't gonna get it."

Most of that relationship drifting was before the height of second-wave feminism, about which Betty knew nothing. She didn't know the patriarchal history of the institution of marriage, which middle-class females of her generation were reading about in women's studies classes and discussing at meetings. She had never encountered the term "patriarchy" (nor had I until I was a young woman in college). She only knew that she wouldn't let a man, town, or boss mistreat her or her children.

Over those years, jobs and locations proved just as impermanent as romance. Betty worked in countless places and drove all over the country with my mother, great-grandmother, and aunts in search of a better place, smoke streaming out of a rattling jalopy's cracked window, a cigarette in the hand that no longer wore a ring.

One might be tempted to speculate that a woman with that sort of resume can't stay put, that it's her nature rather than her circumstances that causes her to find trouble and leave again and again. Maybe even that a lack of self-respect drew her to horrible situations. But that would be underestimating the number of hard hands a young woman in poverty in the 1960s could be dealt in a row.

When Betty finally got dealt a couple good hands, she held onto her cards. Around age 30, she landed a position as a secretary in the Kansas courts system in downtown Wichita. There, she worked her way up the job ladder and remained a state employee for nearly 20 years until her retirement. In her early 30s, when she met the man I grew up knowing as my grandfather — a fun, kind farmer and the first man in her life who had ever treated her right — she married him and lived on his farm for the next 22 years, until his death.

A woman of middle-class means might find herself fighting for parity with men in her corporate office or demanding that her husband change diapers and vacuum; she might organize political meetings, write letters to local newspaper editors demanding her daughter's basketball team receive coverage on par with her son's, donate money to Planned Parenthood, and use some of her hard-earned savings to spend a weekend marching with fellow women in the nation's capital. All these admirable actions involve leveraging some existing sliver of agency within an institution to change it. That middle-class woman is working to improve a woman's place inside the workforce, domestic life, public policy, politics. Those realms have become hospitable enough for her that she might stick around and change them.

For the poor woman, there is much less social, financial, or cultural agency for changing a situation from the inside. But she might have a car and a bit of money for gas, which is enough to leave a situation behind.

Regardless of one's economic lot, there's a powerful wisdom in just leaving the bullshit for someone else to fix. I knew this when I was a professor at a small university with a curious history of tenured female professors resigning. Sometimes even middle-class women, those of us who could stay and try to change the worlds in which we find ourselves, realize we could give our entire lives to shift things an inch. Is the inch worth our lives? I resigned five months after I was tenured.

Several of my middle-class female friends, I could tell, worried I'd lost my mind. At the time, I had no financial security or prospects outside that job. I did have a mortgage and a load of student debt. But my job at that university, I found, involved a daily grind of sexist bullshit not so different in essence from the slaps on the ass I'd gotten for seven years as a waitress. Ultimately, it wasn't gonna get it. Two women who asked no questions, only quietly nodded yes with a deep knowing, were my mom and Grandma Betty.

In that moment, I left the very institution I'd harnessed to climb out of poverty — the same one that separates the strong woman who calls herself a feminist from the strong woman who might be suspicious of the term but embodies it all the same. It turned out to be a very good decision — perhaps the boldest feminist act I will ever make, and one through which dreams came true. I owe the boldness that I tapped to make that decision to the poor woman in my blood. Sometimes a woman who knows her own worth ought to lean in. But sometimes she ought to just leave.

The tension between those two strategies is one Parton would come to know well as Porter Wagoner's young female co-star on a show that bore his name.

Wagoner, who had a string of country hits in the 1950s, was a cunning business force who had leveraged the new television medium before most music artists knew what to do with it. Born in a small town in the Ozarks of southern Missouri, he was a self-made man with an ego that outshone his rhinestone-bedazzled Nudie Cohn suits. He was an imposing physical presence — tall with a long face and serious demeanor, a fake tan, and a yellow pompadour. By contrast, Dolly was five feet tall with a bright, genuine smile and the standard-issue wardrobe of any female singer appearing on television in the 1960s. Parton would become known for flashy looks later in her career, but on Wagoner's show it's clear that he was the one more precious about his appearance.

He was old enough to be her father, but Parton had been hired to be the country-variety-show equivalent of a romantic lead. She was meant to be the pretty thing at his side, singing duets in which man and woman are lovers. But Wagoner would get more than he bargained for.

Initially skeptical of Parton's replacing the former female co-star, Norma Jean, audiences soon adored Parton more than they cared about the host. Both she and Wagoner put out solo records alongside the duets, and hers outsold his. They both wrote songs, and hers were better.

The more threatened Wagoner felt, according to Parton's autobiography, the more tightly he tried to control Parton and her career — telling her what she should sing, what she should write, whether she was allowed to write, who would publish the songs. In her autobiography, Parton recalled feeling wary of conflict. Wagoner was a blustery screamer when he didn't get his way, and hers was a quiet strength; he was a tortured soul who needed his ego puffed up, and she was a stable, empathetic person willing to sacrifice and give a lot. Theirs had the makings of a classic abusive relationship.

Like something out of an abuse playbook, Wagoner did anything he could to push other male business influences out of her life. He shut out her uncle Billy Owens, who had been her musical mentor and industry advocate for years. He insisted she leave her close friend and producer Fred Foster at Monument Records for RCA, where Wagoner acted as an intermediary on the deal. He wanted her to succeed, yes, and her success helped his. As her star rose, though, he became increasingly competitive and possessive.

During a television interview they did together in 1971, which can now be found online, he hooked his long arm around her small shoulders — a classic jealous-boyfriend maneuver many women would recognize — and told her when to speak.

They had no romantic relationship, and Parton has never revealed any direct sexual harassment, but romance rumors inevitably circulate about male and female co-stars. In her autobiography, Parton hinted that Wagoner might have encouraged those rumors — a threatened-co-worker maneuver many women would recognize. Tammy Wynette occasionally filled in for Parton on the show, and Parton recalled Wynette's concern about Wagoner's power to diminish both of their reputations through his tales of sexual conquest.

"One day I was talking to Tammy and she asked me, 'What if Porter claims we all slept with him?'" Parton wrote. "'Don't worry, Tammy,' I said. 'Half of the people will think he's lying and the other half will just think we have bad taste.'"

Parton might have giggled and smiled through Wagoner's power plays, but a close look at their on-screen banter reveals a woman who knows exactly what is happening and will meet every slight with a move at once subtle and capable of dismantling Wagoner's thin veneer of poise.

"You wanna put your guitar away and we'll sing a duet, or you wanna just keep it?" Wagoner asks in one segue into a duet for which he will play guitar. It's delivered in the tone one who lives with a seething personality recognizes as a command rather than a question.

"I'll just hang on to it," Parton says, as if to say, nah, I'm good, you son of a bitch.

"Okay," Wagoner replies through a forced smile.

"I need a security blanket," Parton adds — at once self-deprecating and signaling the boundary of self-preservation she has drawn in that moment. Then Wagoner lays into the strings and they sing "Her and the Car and the Mobile Home," from their 1972 duet album, *The Right Combination — Burning the Midnight Oil*. The song is about a cheating husband returning home to find his suffering wife has left for good.

During the same episode, while introducing a solo performance by Parton, Wagoner makes a joke she doesn't like. From off-camera, she talks back, joke-arguing with what he's said. For a second, his big smile falls.

"Shut up," he says flatly, and then the big smile returns and Parton sings her enduring classic "Tennessee Mountain Home."

Perhaps it's no coincidence that Wagoner's aggression is on full display in that episode from 1972 — the year Parton's five-year contract with him was up. Statistics show that the moment a male abuser is most likely to kill his female partner is at or after the moment she leaves him. Parton has never accused Wagoner of physical violence, but his well-documented emotional manipulation and intimidation are rooted in the same psychology.

Wagoner convinced Parton to stay on past her contract terms, but tension between them only increased. In one particularly barbed exchange during a 1973 episode, there is no mistaking that the sweet girl Wagoner hired is a bold woman who is just about done.

"We're back again," Wagoner says, hooking his arm around Parton's shoulders. "Me and my sidekick here. She just kicked me in the side." Wagoner flinches and gasps to pretend Parton has struck him, and they both smile and laugh.

Parton turns and looks up at his face. "Not yet, but I think I will after that," she says.

Wagoner's arm falls away from her, and his smile falls away from his face — this time for more than just a second.

"Ohhh," he trails in what some viewers might hear as the low, perversely pleased tone an abuser gets when he finds an excuse to unleash his violence. "If you ever hit me and I find it out, Dolly Parton, you'll be in trouble."

Then, within seconds, they are smiling and bobbing through the conversational duet "Run That by Me One More Time," in which a man lies about where he's been and a woman lies about how much money she spent.

At the end of the number, Wagoner summons someone from the audience to join them onstage. It's Jimmy Dean, the country singer — an enormous man who enters the shot as a lumbering blue suit headed for Parton with his arms outstretched. He forces himself onto Parton while she laughs and pushes at him to keep their torsos apart for an uncomfortably long moment. Parton has held her own against Wagoner in a verbal fencing match, only to be physically accosted by a man whose name is synonymous with sausage.

The courage and audacity Parton summoned in those moments might be lost on us today. She wasn't just a professional pioneer for women but one whose shape represented, for men, the ultimate sexual trigger. You can bet she rarely walked into a room in which men didn't fantasize about pinning her body down, and you can bet that when she walked out they claimed they had. It's probably a blessing that she got married so soon after arriving in Nashville; while so many men would disrespect a single woman, some would avoid harassing one who wears a wedding band, whether because they see her as being "claimed" or because her husband might be bigger than they are.

Wagoner, though, was Parton's husband in the public's eye, and the same spunk that was driving him mad helped him turn a massive profit. In the studio recording of "Run That by Me One More Time," Wagoner says at the end, in his speaking voice, "I ought to box your jaws." Parton responds, "Aw, you'd hit your mama before you hit me."

This humorous bravado in the face of an unfunny threat is a signature of female country music and indeed the culture of working-class women. My grandma Betty, you'll recall, really did have her jaw broken by an angry husband as she was leaving him. She was 23, poor with two kids, and he was soon to be her third ex-husband. She told me about it with a laugh.

"Feel this," she said, jutting her chin toward me and putting my hand on it. I felt her lower jaw, as she shifted it to one side and it made a big click, slightly out of joint as it had been for almost 50 years. "That was a gift from one of my sweethearts."

Like so many women, Betty — almost exactly Parton's age — had lived a life more privileged classes sometimes say is "like a country song." What that analysis misses is that artists like Parton intentionally told the stories of the women they knew, otherwise voiceless in society. In other words, the living came before the song. Parton has never strayed from representing them, whether in the lyrics she wrote or the woman she is — who isn't so unlike the woman in "Her and the Car and the Mobile Home," who takes off with the trailer in the end.

Escape Artists

People can be found packing up and leaving in the lyrics of songs in most musical genres, but there is something particularly poor, female, and American about the leaving that happens in

country music. You could think of the woman in these songs as the counterpart to the rambling male outlaw who sings of gambling, honky-tonks, and trains.

The woman those men's lyrics often claim is waiting back home is, in my experience, more like Lorrie Morgan in one of her early-'90s hits: She tells a partner who has taken her for granted and doesn't believe she'll really leave, "watch me," and you can hear in her voice which one of them is right. In "Wrong Side of Memphis," Trisha Yearwood puts a '69 Tempest on Highway 40 and points it toward Nashville to chase her childhood dream of playing the Opry because she's got nothing to lose. Such departures are made possible by the personal freedoms and geographic expanses of the United States that are more often associated with male adventures. (Leaving pervades the broader world of roots music, too. In her two biggest hits, Tracy Chapman skeptically asks for one good reason to stay and plans to leave a hard life behind with a fast car and some money that she saved working at the convenience store.)

The economically hard-up woman is less tethered than the middle-class one, whose survival is more assured and who might have a high-stakes career, a yoga studio membership, a leadership post in the PTA of a suburban school district. The poor woman might have a harder time finding resources for hitting the road, but in spirit she is what they call a flight risk, and what she longs to fly away from is more than just a wayward man. It's a small town, a brutal job at the factory, an entire class.

In "Boston Town," bluegrass band Della Mae speaks as one of the women of the famous 1912 Bread and Roses Strike in Lawrence, Massachusetts, where

nearly 30,000 textile workers, most of them female, immigrant, and ethnically diverse, joined forces to expose dangerous work conditions and demand better wages.

Standing on the floor
In the City of the Spindles.
Got me a job
Lift me up to the middle.

The offering painted
A very pretty picture:
Work at the mills
Held a promise of the Scripture.

But a girl like me was worked
to the bone.
Your fingers bled and your
body moaned.
Fourteen hours a day,
and then my paycheck was
half of the men's.

Looking down with oppression's face,
that pile of money they
steal and waste.
Then they said they'd have
to cut our pay,
so we broke our cage and
formed the FLRA.

They said what a waste of a pretty girl
to let the labor flag unfurl.
I said what more can you
take from me?
I own my hands and my dignity.

"Boston Town" is a rare overt political statement in roots music, but uncommon in any genre is the exaltation of working-class female strength at the root of social change — which is precisely what many of Parton's early songs are about. She just tells them at the ground level, in the

Like so many women, Betty — almost exactly Parton's age — had lived a life more privileged classes sometimes say is "like a country song." What that analysis misses is that artists like Parton intentionally told the stories of the women they knew, otherwise voiceless in society. In other words, the living came before the song.

hearts and homes of women.

Interestingly, Parton's songs aren't about women freeing themselves from oppressive situations. The female escape artist we find in modern roots music reflects political, social, and cultural progress, if only for a woman perceiving her ability to leave. Parton's early songwriting captures the moment just before that progress, though. Hers are not tales about cars and horizons but rather dark, minor-key acknowledgments of situations a woman might need to escape. Over and over, young Parton sings about women who are stuck in a place of cultural and economic subjugation.

Parton's first hit with RCA, 1968's "Just Because I'm a Woman," illuminated the sexual double standards that encouraged men to be playboys but morally incriminated the women who slept with them. The song follows a standard country-guitar strum, but the ideas Parton pushed through Nashville in the lyrics were as revolutionary as the feminist publications coming out of academia and radical small presses. The song describes "slut shaming" long before that was a term:

> I can see you're disappointed
> By the way you look at me
> And I'm sorry that I'm not
> The woman you thought I'd be.
>
> Yes, I've made my mistakes
> But listen and understand
> My mistakes are no worse than yours
> Just because I'm a woman.
>
> So when you look at me
> Don't feel sorry for yourself.
> Just think of all the shame

> You might have brought
> somebody else.
>
> Just let me tell you this
> Then we'll both know where we stand.
> My mistakes are no worse than yours
> Just because I'm a woman.
>
> Now a man will take a good girl
> And he'll ruin her reputation.
> But when he wants to marry
> Well, that's a different situation.
>
> He'll just walk off and leave her
> To do the best she can
> While he looks for an angel
> To wear his wedding band.

Parton has said she got the idea for the song from her own life. She had grown up feeling sexually precocious and free in the backwoods of Tennessee, she wrote in her autobiography. She had a domineering Pentecostal preacher for a grandfather and was cast as a Jezebel for wearing tight clothes and smudging a burnt matchstick around her lashes as eyeliner, but she had somewhere liberated herself without any impetus other than her own desires and beliefs.

When she met her husband, Carl Dean, at a laundromat in Nashville just after getting to town, he promptly decided they were meant to get hitched and apparently assumed a woman as nice as Dolly must also be a "nice girl." Eight months after their wedding, he decided to ask if she'd been with other men before him.

"I assumed it didn't matter," she told Entertainment Weekly in 2009. "... I figured the truth was better, because I didn't want to start a marriage with a lie." The news crushed him, and he moped

around about it for months.

"He could not get over that for the longest time," she told Rolling Stone in 2003. "I thought, 'Well, my goodness, what's the big damn deal?'"

To her great satisfaction, the song she got out of that marital conflict reached the top-20 chart in South Africa a few years after its US release. "All those oppressed women!" she exclaimed about it in the Rolling Stone profile.

Parton continued to challenge the false saint-or-whore dichotomy with the title track of her 1975 release "The Bargain Store," which Wagoner co-produced with Bob Ferguson at RCA. In the song, a haunting but self-assured plea from a woman to her would-be lover, a woman compares herself to merchandise that has been used and even damaged but is nonetheless still in good-enough condition. The bold chorus might even reference more than just an open heart: "The bargain store is open — come inside."

Parton recalled in the Entertainment Weekly interview that "a lot of stations wouldn't play it because they thought it was about a whore." The single nonetheless climbed the charts to be her fifth number-one solo song.

Parton's 1970 album, The Fairest of Them All, recorded about halfway through her time on The Porter Wagoner Show, is made of Parton originals that bear witness to the horrors endured by women at the physical and economic mercy of men and their desires. The album title references that most sexist of fairy tales, of course; on the cover, Parton smiles into a mirror with the fresh face of Snow White, but her pink ruff evokes the wicked queen.

In "Daddy Come and Get Me," a grown daughter begs her father to rescue her from a mental institution where her husband has committed her so that he can be with another woman. That song shed light on the centuries-old practice of branding a sane woman "crazy" and institutionalizing her when it suited someone else's narrative, still a phenomenon in psychiatry in the 1970s.

On the third track of Fairest, a woman tells her lover that she will leave if he tries to change or control her. "I'll be movin' on when possession gets too strong," Parton sings.

In "I'm Doing This for Your Sake," a woman's heart breaks as she tells a baby she must give it up for adoption since the father ran off; he promised her they'd get married to get her into bed and then split once he heard she was pregnant.

The songwriting jewel of the album, "Down from Dover," sounds like pop-country in 1970: steel guitar, tambourine, backup vocals, a bit of harpsichord layered against a mid-tempo guitar melody. But it's classic Parton storytelling from that early point in her career, when the ghosts of the women's fates she has escaped are still close at her heels. In the story, a teenage girl gets pregnant and is shamed and kicked out of the house by her parents. The baby's father has left town, giving her a line that he'll be back to marry her before she starts showing. She prays for the boy to return, but seasons change without any word. In autumn, she goes into labor alone and delivers a stillborn daughter without medical help:

I guess in some strange way she knew
She'd never have a father's arms
to hold her.
And dying was her way
of telling me he wasn't
coming down from Dover.

The song remains one of Parton's favorites, she has said, and was covered by Marianne Faithfull and Nancy Sinatra. Just a few years before she recorded it, she had been smiling and bobbing to "Dumb Blonde" — a song written by a man, conveying some sass but lacking the darkness Parton brought with her from Sevier County's hollers. Now, she was telling gothic stories about women that were too true to even get played on the radio. RCA wouldn't release "Dover" as a single.

"There's no way we can put out a single about a woman having a baby out of wedlock," Parton would recall studio executives saying. She'd written the song when she was just 18, she has told crowds when introducing the number, but she would be in her 30s before society was ready to watch her sing it.

"It was just a story about a girl havin' a baby — nothin' that really unnatural about that," she told a 1983 London audience. "She thought somebody loved her, he left her in trouble, and never came back — but that seemed to be too heavy at the time."

In the '60s and '70s, Parton had left home for the lights of Nashville and found success. But, in some ways, she was just as trapped as she would have been as a knocked-up kid in a shack in Sevier County. She was one of few female country music stars at the time, all produced and controlled by men in suits. It was such a man's world that she learned golf to keep in their loop. According to her book, once she shot a birdie on a par three hole and was so proud she wanted to have the Titleist ball mounted. Wagoner said he would do it and then gave her a plaque with an Arnold Palmer ball instead, which Parton described as one of his many passive-aggressive digs.

No, Parton hadn't gotten tied down by some careless boy and a teenage pregnancy back in the woods. Instead, she wound up professionally and contractually bound to a man who fancied himself her husband, her father, her owner. That man happened to be her male counterpart in some ways — a talented, tenacious country kid with a guitar who worked hard and hit it big. What she'd stepped into was the wealthier, show-business parallel of a life she'd meant to escape. Her songs from that period thus don't reflect the triumph of an individualistic woman who "got out" but rather the sorrows of women who weren't so lucky — at once a powerful statement of solidarity with her poor sisters back home and a coded revelation of all the things she has never told us about Porter Wagoner.

As Parton toured the country singing those songs, her bus might have passed women's protests, marches, sit-ins. Parton knew little of that world — direct political activism, an understanding of one's own agency in democracy, the way government works, statistics and testimonies leveraged to change public policy. She did know what my grandma Betty knew: female life as a personal, intimate experience in which, at some point, an inner vibration you've been putting off will shake you so hard you'll fall to pieces if you don't leave.

That knowledge is something society will try to squash, because women who don't stay put cannot be controlled. All the institutions benefit if they stay: The heterosexual marriage, for which they carry laundry baskets and the emotional labor. The underpaying jobs, where they do their assigned tasks and are expected to organize the birthday cupcakes in the meeting room, too. The parenting, in which they still change most of the diapers regardless of who "brings home the bacon" — and they still fry most of the bacon, too.

"Stay," her small town seemed to tell Parton when she left Tennessee in 1964, if only by pressuring her to become a wife and mother and laughing at her big ideas about becoming a star. "Stay," Porter Wagoner was telling her a decade later, in plain legal terms. In many ways that remains the message for women everywhere, but today we can revel in songs about departure — songs that tell stories that now feel possible because of the bold departures women before us made.

Many of those departures — especially by the poor woman, the black woman, the brown woman, the gay woman, the transgender woman, the person who wants to live as neither man nor woman — have gone unsung while more privileged people hold forth about equality at microphones next to capital buildings.

Dolly Parton had a different kind of microphone, and a woman her age named Betty was listening. I found Betty's old records when I was a kid, marked in pen with last names I didn't know she'd ever had. I was a child with ideas about leaving, and no one in my family or rural communities ever laughed when I said as much or tried to tell me that I couldn't. No one talked about "feminism" where I lived. But poor girls before me had already worn a groove in the highway.

An Open Door

Considering Parton's years with Wagoner brought to mind the first line from a famous 1978 poem by Adrienne Rich: "A wild patience has taken me this far." In that poem, by one of the country's eminent public intellectuals and second-wave feminists, the middle-aged speaker realizes her deepest strength is that she contains seemingly opposing attributes at once: anger and tenderness, a sad past and hope for the future, both pride and pain from having done a lifetime worth of work alone.

How can patience be wild? It is a question not unlike, "Why would a strong woman put up with it?" The latter insinuates that a strong woman wouldn't. But the fact is that, at least temporarily, almost every woman must.

For Parton, there was the economic stability that had come from her business partnership with Wagoner. She was scandalously underpaid, of course. Like many working women today, though, on some level she was grateful and shocked to be paid at all.

"The jingles were sung, the smiles were faked, and the checks were cashed," Parton said in her autobiography. "Try to imagine what sixty thousand dollars represented to a young woman who had grown up in poverty in the Smoky Mountains. It was probably more than my daddy had earned in his lifetime."

Parton's first Christmas after she got the job on Wagoner's show, she re-did her parents' house with new furniture, drapes, carpet. Her younger siblings were still at home, and she made sure the girls had lots of pink and frilly things Parton had longed for as a child. This concept of "girl stuff" might offend feminist thinking. The rub for Parton wasn't that such things were forced on her, though, but that she couldn't have them. In a place where women worked their fingers to the bone right alongside men, with no money for makeup or dresses even if they wanted them, pink ruffles weren't just a gender performance but an economic privilege.

(For the record, the first big purchase she made for herself once she was thoroughly wealthy wasn't girly stuff. It was a Cadillac.)

Grandma Betty never got rich or even became what most people would consider "comfortable," but her job in the Kansas criminal justice system eventually provided enough that she could cover the bills while a small pension grew. When I was a kid, she had an emerald ring she always wore, and one day I asked her who had given it to her.

"I've had it since I started working in the courts," she told me. "I always wanted an emerald ring, so I bought the damn thing myself." She didn't need to explain to me the significance — that every other ring she'd put on a finger came from a man.

Through her gig on Wagoner's show, Parton got more than financial security. She racked up awards that had both their names on them — in 1968, they won the Country Music Association's honor for vocal group of the year. And Wagoner could be a real advocate for her when he wanted to be. Though their connection became strained, like most abusive relationships it had its charms and good moments.

In 1970, Wagoner orchestrated "Dolly Parton Day" back in her hometown, bringing top Nashville

musicians to Sevierville for the event. The performance was recorded for the essential live album *A Real Live Dolly*. Wagoner profited from that seemingly selfless tribute to Parton and her roots, of course, but by her account he had a genuine affection and respect for her, too. It was mutual.

"He was a Missouri boy with a dream," she wrote in her autobiography. Their life trajectories were so rare that they understood each other as few others were capable of understanding either one of them.

Wagoner could be a good teacher, too. By the time they became partners, she'd been working professionally for almost 20 years, since childhood, but next to him, a 20-something woman before a national audience, she still had a lot to learn.

"I could sing when I met Porter," Parton wrote. "After knowing him, I knew how to perform."

He taught her how to handle a ruckus in the audience; you can still see his mark on a Parton show today when someone interrupts a quiet moment with a shout and she throws back a line such as "I thought I told you to wait in the truck."

Parton might have gotten her eye for rhinestones and over-the-top hair from Wagoner; today you're more likely to see her in a Nudie suit or something similarly bejeweled than in the demure dresses she wore when she started on the show.

Perhaps the most important impression Wagoner made on her, though, had to do with fans.

"Every night after performing on the road, no matter how small the town or seemingly insignificant the venue, Porter would stay and sign autographs until the last fan who wanted one had been satisfied," Parton recalled in her book.

As it happens, it was during one of those dedicated autograph sessions that she would have an encounter that paved the way for her to leave Porter Wagoner. It was a little girl, nine or ten years old, holding out a piece of paper to be signed. Parton admired her long, auburn hair.

"You sure are pretty," Parton would recall saying. "What's your name?"

"Jolene," the girl said.

Parton had never heard that name before. She remembered it a year later when, according to her, she sat down to write a song inspired by a flirtatious connection between her husband and

an auburn-haired woman who worked at their bank. She needed a name for the character of the woman who represented a threat. The name she picked, plucked from that young fan she met while on the road with Wagoner, turned out to have such a ring to it that countless musicians across genres would cover the song for decades.

The 1973 single "Jolene" went to number one on the country charts, was a crossover pop success, and was nominated for a Grammy. It wasn't her first solo triumph, but something about the moment felt different: Parton was emboldened. She had been patient over her years with Wagoner but never lost her own wild spirit. Despite the big smiles on camera and onstage, the pair had gone round and round behind the scenes.

"That was not unique to Porter," Parton wrote. "I had seldom agreed with parents, teachers, anybody who tried to exercise control over me, my talents, and my beliefs."

Ultimately, they had different visions — he wanted to keep her, and she wasn't for being kept.

"I guess the real problems that arose between Porter and me were all about dueling dreams," Parton wrote. "Porter dreamed of me staying with his show forever, and I dreamed of having my own show."

By then, she had stayed on two years past her five-year contractual obligation, apparently from a sense of obligation to a man who claimed she owed him her career. Parton is not one to complain about or elaborate on her relationship with Wagoner as anything more than a blessing that often felt like a pain in the ass. But her jokes about those years, like the songs written during them, have a darkness to them.

"Looking back, it seems appropriate," she wrote of the time she stayed with Wagoner. "After all, the indentured servants who came to the New World had to work seven years for their freedom."

So in her late 20s, a decade after she left rural East Tennessee, she once again found the gumption to leave something that no longer served her purposes. They were on the road, touring as the longtime duet, Parton recalled in her book. There was a taxi in front of the hotel with the door opened for her.

"My knees nearly buckled, my heart nearly stopped, but I walked on," she wrote.

"When that car door closed, I knew it

work. Her bittersweet goodbye, thus, was something she owned and that Wagoner had no claim on. Every penny it earned fell into her account, not his.

Her first summer away from Wagoner, Parton hit the road to open for Mac Davis. I imagine her rolling down the highway with her new band Gypsy Fever in a bus with butterflies and her first name painted on the side. Riding along might have been Don Warden, the legendary (and recently deceased) steel guitarist who was from Wagoner's hometown and had been part of his show and original trio. He and Parton had become close, and when she left Wagoner, so did he, to work as her manager for almost half a century.

Parton must have felt a new lightness as the bus zoomed past a field she wasn't working in, a diner where she would never have to wait tables. She was 28 and free for the first time in her life, no place or man or contract pinning her wings. I imagine "I Will Always Love You" coming on the bus radio, the Gypsy Fever members cheering when the DJ announces it had hit number one on the charts. I imagine the 1972 Carly Simon hit "You're So Vain" playing next and Parton singing along, laughing her ass off at one particular line in the chorus: "I'll bet you think this song is about you, don't you?"

When Elvis Presley asked to record "I Will Always Love You," Parton was ecstatic, she recalled in a 2006 interview with CMT. She was a star by then, but Presley was already an icon. Then, at the last minute before the recording session, Presley's manager, the legendary "Colonel" Tom Parker, tried to pull a business maneuver on her.

"He said, 'Now you know we have a rule that Elvis don't record anything that we don't take half the publishing,'" Parton told CMT. "And I was really quiet. I said, 'Well, now it's already been a hit. I wrote it and I've already published it. And this is the stuff I'm leaving for my family when I'm dead and gone.'"

Parker told her it was deal or no deal.

"I guess they thought since they already had it prepared and already had it ready, that I would do it," Parton mused. "I said, 'I'm really sorry,' and I cried all night. ... Other people were saying, 'You're nuts. It's Elvis Presley. I mean, hell, I'd give him all of it.'"

But Parton went with her gut. It would prove one of the most lucrative decisions of her life.

was the end of an era. One Dolly Parton had walked so painfully to the car and climbed inside; another stronger one had closed the door."

One of her concerns was that RCA wouldn't want her anymore. Wagoner, working cleverly as a go-between, had insinuated the label wasn't interested in her without him. She asked for a conference in New York and met with executive juggernauts Ken Glancy and Mel Ilberman.

"I know I'm not the same without Porter," she recalled telling them, "but I'll be something really special by myself." According to Parton, they were shocked.

"We're somewhat interested in maintaining a relationship with Porter Wagoner, but we think you are the real star," they said, and she couldn't believe it.

It's hard to imagine a woman who built a business empire being so nervous. It is no surprise, though, that she wouldn't know the world valued her as much as she valued herself. However strong you are, years of feedback from an emotional manipulator like Wagoner will do a number on your mind.

To mark her departure from the show, Parton wrote the tearjerker goodbye song "I Will Always Love You" and told Wagoner it was for him — her genius channeled as a testament to him and their relationship.

A song that powerful doesn't get written without truth behind every word. But consider what a goodbye in that form represented. No dummy, Parton had long ago established a song publishing company and retained the rights whenever someone recorded her

"I Will Always Love You" went to number one again when Parton re-recorded it in 1982, making it the only country song in history to top the charts in two separate decades. The song did it again in 1992, when Whitney Houston made it a pop blockbuster on *The Bodyguard* soundtrack. Thus, Parton's parting gift to the man who would have held her down ended up one of the most successful songs in music history. She is still cashing the checks.

"When Whitney's [version] came out, I made enough money to buy Graceland," Parton told CMT with a laugh.

The confidence to heed to her inner voice and, in doing so, piss off a powerful man is what allowed Parton to leave Wagoner, say no to Elvis, and become not just a successful artist but also a business juggernaut.

"You need to really believe in what you've got to offer, what your talent is — and if you believe, that gives you strength," Parton told *Billboard* magazine in 2014. "In my early days, I would go in, and I was always over-made, with my boobs sticking out, my clothes too tight, and so I really looked like easy prey to a lot of guys — just looked easy, period. But I would go in, and if they were not paying close attention to what I was saying, I always said, 'I look like a woman, but I think like a man and you better pay attention or I'll have your money and I'll be gone.'"

Gone she was, and Wagoner responded in predictable fashion — with a bitter lawsuit. He claimed that, having played such a big role in her development, he was owed a cut of every profit she'd make for the rest of her life as an entertainer. That would seem like a losing claim today, maybe, but Parton probably had fair reason for concern as a woman facing the prospect of a courtroom with a male judge. Rather than fight Wagoner in court, Parton offered to settle for a reported $1 million. Wagoner took the deal.

According to Parton's book, she didn't yet have that amount lying around and paid it off painstakingly over time. Meanwhile, Wagoner was slandering her name any chance he could get.

"Dolly Parton is the kind of person that I would never trust with anything of mine," Wagoner told a TV interviewer in 1978. "I mean her family, her own blood, she would turn her back on to help herself. I'm not that kind of person."

It must have been hard for him to cope with the fact that Parton's star had so thoroughly eclipsed his that, according to *People* magazine, she sometimes bailed him out of tax trouble.

Parton and Wagoner would reconcile and reunite many times over the decades, even poking fun at their history together. At a 1995 roast of Wagoner, Parton told the crowd, "I knew he had balls when he sued me for a million dollars when he was only paying me 30 dollars a week."

Parton would continue to reflect on Wagoner with a mix of straight talk and gracious thanks over the years.

"I will always be grateful to Porter, because I learned a lot," she told *Rolling Stone* in 2003. "But he got as much out of me as I got out of him, let's put it that way. Porter was very much like my dad and my brothers and the men I grew up with. They were just manly men, and a woman's place was where you told her to be. And so I would always stand up to him. Because I had my own talent. I didn't come here just to be the girl singer on Porter Wagoner's show. And we fought like hell, and he showed his ass about it, rather than just letting life flow. He had to sue me. And, of course, that broke both our hearts. And, you know, looking back on it now, he hates that he did that and has said so."

Parton and Wagoner might have buried the hatchet, but the social forces that created the gender and economic inequities between them are still going strong. Consider this bit of writing by a music critic for *The New York Times* in 2007, which reads like a passage from a hagiographic biography Wagoner might have commissioned in the 1970s:

"For all Mr. Wagoner's accomplishments, he could not escape a certain question. 'Did you sing with Dolly?' too many people asked.

"'No,' he would say with a smile. 'She sang with me.'"

Punching Out

As Parton was leaving Wagoner, feminist activism was changing the world. The Supreme Court ruled on Roe v. Wade, which might have saved so many of the young, pregnant, abandoned protagonists of Parton's early songs, in 1973. The next year, it became illegal to force a pregnant woman to take maternity leave based on the idea she was incapable of working, and the Women's Educational Equity Act funded development of less sexist teaching materials.

While many of those gains have been lasting, America did not emerge into some brighter moment for women, on the whole. Reproductive rights, in particular, have been the target of nationwide, death-by-a-thousand-cuts operations led by college-educated white men for decades.

Similarly, though freed from her chains to Wagoner, Parton did not find herself in a pat, happy ending. A woman can leave the poor countryside and a domineering male boss, but she can't leave a culture of sexism and misogyny. Mindfully reject it every single day with some success? Perhaps. But live outside it? No.

To say nothing of battles she surely fought behind closed doors, Parton's songwriting would continue to outrage powerful men well past the moment at which equality had supposedly been reached. Her 1991 song "Eagle When She Flies," a ballad she wrote to pay homage to the simultaneous vulnerability and deep power of women, had trouble getting on the airwaves just like "Down from Dover" and "The Bargain Store" had a quarter century prior.

"Lots of DJs wouldn't play [it] because they thought it was such a women's lib song," Parton recalled in the 2003 *Rolling Stone* interview.

That Parton herself didn't affix the label "women's lib" to her own work tells you where she came from. But the fact that men decided her song shouldn't be heard tells you exactly what it was. Some working-class women might be hesitant about a movement that they feel kept outside of, suspicious of words from a language they didn't get to learn. But even if feminism is not in their talk, it's in their walk.

Here was Parton's walk in response to male DJs chucking "Eagle When She Flies": She performed it at the Country Music Association Awards with president George H.W. Bush and First Lady Barbara Bush in the front row. She took the opportunity to introduce her song using no less than the ultimate symbol of patriarchy — the rich, white, male leader of the world — as a contrast with what she hoped to exalt.

"Everybody was talkin' about how proud we are to have the president here. And we are. Very honored. But I wanted to do a song tonight, and I want to dedicate this to Barbara Bush," Parton said, her platinum wig almost as high as some of her old beehives and her neckline much lower than what Porter Wagoner would have approved. "We know there are some wonderful men in this world, but there are equally as many great women. She and people like her and women from all walks of life. ... So this is for all the women here tonight and everywhere."

The stage lit up to reveal a large, mostly white choir in cheesy outfits representing professional trades women were newly entering — the businesswoman in shoulder pads, the delivery driver in a brown jumpsuit holding a box, the soldier in fatigues, the astronaut, the policewoman, the surgeon in green scrubs, the construction worker in a hardhat, even a movie director. The old jobs that had previously been deemed appropriate for women were there, too — the teacher, the nurse, the female rancher, the diner waitress with her tray. But the president of the United States of America, a man who had everything handed to him while Parton earned hers, had to consider the visuals. Captive before cameras in the front row, he had to sit there while the daughter of an illiterate farmer told him his wife was his equal. It was an exquisite demonstration that still feels radical when you watch it in 2017.

That was almost 30 years after Parton left Sevierville, Tennessee, as a teenager with a guitar. Sexual discrimination in the workplace was by then against the law, and many more women were recording country music. In some ways, during the quarter century since that CMA Awards performance, women have made even more progress. But I worry that such progress is most often attributed to the efforts of mostly white middle-class or affluent women who may speak the right words but not necessarily live up to their own ideals.

Some of us get so lost in the discussion of feminism that we fail to look ruthlessly at the way we live our lives, ask what sort of country songs might be written about us. Would they be about the woman who is stuck or the one breaking free?

You might know a well-off woman with a college degree and a friendly, philandering husband who pays the bills but treats her like a trophy or a maid whether she has her own job or not. She might be comfortable enough in her life to remain. She might even be wearing a T-shirt that reads "feminist" when she goes to yoga class and picks up her husband's dry cleaning. She might know movement terminology that a poor woman can't define, and she might type an outraged post on Facebook about our misogynistic president. Meanwhile, a woman in poverty, who has not once in her life heard the word "misogyny," is walking out some door with nothing to her name, to start over yet again, in the hopes that she and her children will find some goddamn respect. This is an oversimplified hypothetical. But the woman who speaks about feminism is not always the one truly insisting on equality.

Whether penniless Dolly Parton refusing to stay in a holler or affluent Dolly Parton looking at the door of Porter Wagoner's studio, leaving is a revolutionary act with profound economic risk. But leaving is the thing. For obvious reasons, I know poor women to be the more reliable experts on departure. It's an expertise that came in handy for Parton once she found herself in the professional equivalent of being married to a rich asshole. It's a power that has, occasionally over the years, brought textile mills and coal companies and rich corporations to their knees when gender and poverty intersect and working women have had enough.

I recall the thrill I felt as a child watching an episode of *Roseanne* in which the title character stands up to a sexist, verbally abusive boss who goes back on his word and reinstates brutal production quotas for female employees at a plastics plant in small-town Illinois.

"You'll stay ... and so will your loser friends," the boss tells her. After some hot words, Roseanne storms back to the factory floor.

"Hey, I'm not done with you!" he yells and follows her back to where the other women are moving plastic pieces. "Roseanne, I thought I told you not to walk away from me."

"I'm walking away from you forever," she says, her voice soft like she is scared. "I'm walking away from this stinking factory. I'm walking away from this lousy job." Roseanne punches her timecard.

"Well that was a wonderful performance, Roseanne," he says. "If any of you are considering joining her, may I point out there are two doors to this room. One that pays, and one that doesn't."

One by one, her friends of different races and ages stand up and punch their cards.

When Parton punched her card and walked out of the Porter Wagoner music factory, she was helping make a path for female artists in an industry where they still rarely headlined a show.

"There was Patsy Cline and Loretta and Tammy and me," Parton told *Rolling Stone*. "There were just very few of us, and they were all under the direction of men."

You might have seen that list of names before in big letters on a trendy T-shirt sometimes worn by young women being sold feminism not just as a careful doctrine but as a brand. "Dolly & Loretta & Patsy & Tammy," the shirt reads.

When you see it, if you're able, consider giving a big tip to the next woman who serves you at a diner like the ones on the Great Plains where my grandma waited tables, or to the cleaning lady carrying a bucket on and off Greyhound buses like Patsy Cline used to do down South. Feminism owes her a debt, and there's a good chance she's saving up to get somewhere. Her life isn't the kind you want to lean into. ∎

Contributors

ALISON BROWN is a Grammy-winning banjoist who fronts the Alison Brown Quartet. She is also the co-founder of Compass Records. Her latest album is *The Song of the Banjo* (2015).

CARA GIBNEY writes about music for *No Depression*, *fRoots*, Americana UK, *CultureHub* magazine, *Gigging NI*, and elsewhere. She lives in Belfast, Ireland.

COLIN SUTHERLAND is an illustrator and designer living in the mountains of North Carolina. He finds inspiration in century-old fiddle tunes, vintage print ephemera, and the bawl of his bluetick coonhound.

CORBIE HILL is a freelance writer who lives on three wooded acres in Pittsboro, North Carolina, with his wife and two daughters. His work appears in the *News & Observer, INDY Week*, and a handful of other papers and magazines, though if he had it all to do over again he'd be a scientist.

DAVE WILSON is the guitarist, primary songwriter, and lead singer of North Carolina-based stringband Chatham County Line.

DENIS GAINTY was a mandolin player and associate professor of history at Georgia State University in Atlanta. He was writing a book on the history of bluegrass music in Japan before he passed away in early 2017.

DREW CHRISTIE is a Seattle-based animator and illustrator. His work has been featured by *The New York Times, Huffington Post, The Atlantic*, and others.

HILARY SAUNDERS is the assistant music editor at *Paste* magazine, as well as a full-time freelance writer. She's written about arts and culture for publications around the world and is an unironic believer that rock and roll can save the world.

JILL KETTLES is a publicist with a bad photography habit who loves her cats, singing in the car, and eating Honey Nut Cheerios for all three meals. She is self-taught on the camera, art school-trained on the canvas, and can pitch a pair of dirty socks to the media with pride.

JODY AMABLE is a writer based in the San Francisco Bay Area whose work has been seen in The Bay Bridged, Metro newspapers, and Ravishly. She lives in San Jose with her accordion, a record collection, and a dog she loves more than most people.

JUSTIN JOFFE is a Brooklyn-based journalist covering music, art, media, and technology. He has written for numerous publications including *Spin, Noisey, Relix*, and *Flaunt*. He's a full-time contributor to *Observer*'s arts section.

KIM RUEHL is a recovering songwriter who unexpectedly landed in a job as a music writer in 2005. Since then, her work has been published in *Billboard, Yes, Seattle Weekly*, NPR, and elsewhere. She's the editor-in-chief of *No Depression* and, these days, uses her songwriting skills to improv showtunes for her 3-year-old daughter. She lives in Asheville, North Carolina, with her family.

LEE ZIMMERMAN has been a freelance writer for publications like *American Songwriter, Blurt*, and *Billboard* for 20 years. He lives in Maryville, Tennessee, with his wife.

MARY GAUTHIER is a singer-songwriter and an author. She's released seven studio albums and is currently under contract with Yale University Press for a book on songwriting due out in 2017.

MATT POWELL is a writer and musician from Los Angeles. He plays guitar in the Incredible Heavies, and learned many of life's lessons managing the Ernest Tubb Record Shop on Nashville's Lower Broad.

MEGAN ROMER moved from Upstate New York to South Louisiana over a decade ago, and has been writing professionally ever since. Her writing focuses on the hyper-local cultural abundance she finds every time she steps out the door.

SAMUEL J. FELL is an Australian freelance journalist and writer. He's a critic for the *Sydney Morning Herald* and *Rolling Stone*, and contributes to a range of publications covering music, politics and travel. His first book, *Stars & Hype: First Time Notes on the American Deep South*, was published in late 2016.

SARAH SMARSH is a journalist who writes about socioeconomic class in America. She has reported on public policy for *Harper's*, NewYorker.com, *The Guardian, Guernica*, and others. Her essays on cultural boundaries have been published by *Aeon, McSweeney's*, and more. She formerly reviewed female country acts for alt-weeklies in the Midwest. Smarsh's book on the working poor and her upbringing in rural Kansas is forthcoming from Scribner. She lives in Kansas and Texas.

STACY CHANDLER is the assistant editor of *No Depression*. She is a freelance writer and editor living in Raleigh, North Carolina, with her husband, their daughter, a big dumb yellow dog, and an underused fiddle.

ZOYE RUEHL is a consummate Millennial who loves all the music, drinks all the coffee, designs shoes, and studies industrial and accessory design at Savannah College of Art and Design.

NO DEPRESSION

PART OF THE FRESHGRASS FOUNDATION

No Depression is brought to you by the FreshGrass Foundation, a 501(c)(3) nonprofit organization dedicated to preserving and promoting the past, present, and future of American roots music. In addition to publishing *No Depression* and presenting the annual FreshGrass Festival at Mass MoCA in Western Massachusetts each September, the Foundation funds cash awards for up-and-coming musicians, the *No Depression* Singer-Songwriter Award, the *No Depression* Writing Fellow, and more. Visit freshgrass.org for more information

Fall 2017: Foremothers

For much of the history of American roots music, women were not allowed to travel and perform unless they were accompanied by a husband, father, or brother. For some time, it was even considered radical to have a woman fronting a performing group. Yet there have always been women music-makers pulling traditional music forward — consider Maybelle and Sara with the Carter Family, Dolly Parton, Emmylou Harris, Hazel & Alice, and so many others. This issue digs into the deep roots of the women who laid the foundation for American roots music, from the perspective of ND's finest writers as well as musicians themselves.

Included in this issue:

Dolly Parton, Emmylou Harris, and Linda Ronstadt / Ruthie Foster / Karen Dalton / Annie Oakley / Elizabeth Cotten / Maybelle and Sara Carter and The Carter Sisters / Alice Gerrard / Bonnie Bramlett / art by Caitlin Cary, and more

Winter 2017: Singer-Songwriters

Included in this issue:

Ani DiFranco / Jackson Browne / Josh Ritter / Hayes Carll / Rhiannon Giddens / Colin Hay / Honey Dewdrops / Susan Werner / Sarah Shook / Dan Bern / Danny Schmidt & Carrie Elkin / Birds of Chicago / Woody Guthrie, Pete Seeger, and Phil Ochs / Father John Misty, Conor Oberst, Jason Isbell, and more

Spring 2018: Music and Place

Explore the stories behind songs about railroads, coal mines, farms, union halls, battleships, cities, small towns, rivers, mountains, and more. What does roots music have to do with the place where it was written and made? The answer: So much.

Summer 2018: TBA

NODEPRESSION.COM/SUBSCRIBE

Photos by Mary Gauthier, from her various tours of Europe.

Screen Door

WHAT A TRAVELING SONGWRITER KNOWS ABOUT HUMAN NATURE

BY MARY GAUTHIER

I make my living on the road, traveling in circles — town to town, country to country, year after year — mostly by myself. In any given year, I play over a hundred shows, and over the last two decades, I've performed in dozens of countries. I've stayed in homes, hostels, hotels, motels, inns, B&Bs, and rooming houses all over the world. As an internationally touring singer-songwriter, I've come to learn that while each nation has its unique characteristics, human nature is universal.

My travels have shown me that when we see ourselves in a song, we know that we are not removed from everyone else, not emotionally unique. Songs act on us like an ancient, wise, intuitive medicine. They are not unlike the mechanisms in our body that race to a wound to begin healing. But instead of healing our physical bodies, songs heal our spirit, our soul, and lift us up emotionally, even when the song is sad.

Songs create soul bridges — metaphysical planks across emotional divides. They help the songwriter cross the abyss that separates her from herself, and they help the listener do the same. Singing songs together connects us as a people, reassuring us that we are not alone.

In all my travels, following my songs around the world, I've learned that there is no such thing as an ordinary life. That resonance with other humans is humanity's deepest desire. And an emotionally true song resonates to the core — to the most essential part of us.

I've played my songs unplugged in front of farmers, standing on a handmade stage in a hay-filled barn in the Black Forest of Germany. I've played on a gambling boat in Frankfurt

(cigarette smoking was allowed and, good Lord, it was smoky), singing my songs as we chugged around the Rhine-Main-Danube connector, passing other brightly lit gambling boats as we sailed in circles for two hours.

I've stayed in the Reeperbahn "entertainment" district in Hamburg, where rooms rent by the hour and the sex trade flourishes. There, I performed in a filthy, run-down rock club across the boulevard from the Star Club, where The Beatles woodshedded in their early days.

I've played shows in Dresden, in the former East Germany, right after the wall came down. I stayed in the former East Berlin, in a low-budget hotel called the East/West Inn, in full view of the graffiti-filled tumbling wall. There, I learned that art knows no borders. It transcends human boundaries.

I've played near the sea grass by the ocean, next to the Iron Cross that marks the forced removal of the Acadian people by the British in the Eastern Canadian Maritime province of Nova Scotia, Grand Prix. I sang "Mercy Now" at the site of the expulsion that led to the Acadian "trail of tears," known in French-speaking Canada as Le Grand

Dérangement. There and elsewhere, I learned that songs heal. They are pieces of the soul, reaching through eternity, to heal the heart. They make us feel and believe that we are not alone.

I played at the International Townes Van Zandt festival in Figino, Serenza, Italy, where dozens of musicians from all over Europe came together to celebrate the music of the late Texas songwriter. There I saw that songs are the great connectors of our time, the true international language — the language of the heart. After all, at our center, we are the same. Songs are road maps into strangers' hearts, which upon inspection, mirror our own.

I played a show in Trondheim, Norway, in the country's maximum-security prison, which was was nothing at all like an American maximum-security prison. In Norway, they don't even call them prisons. They are called hospitals, and there are no guards. Instead, there are doctors and nurses, and everyone wears street clothes. I couldn't tell the patients (inmates?) from the staff.

I've played in the attic of a frozen-in-time 18th century sail-maker's workshop outside Bergen, Norway, with the craftsman's tools just as he left them when he died at the end of the last century. I've performed in a mirrored red Belgian burlesque carnival tent at the Tønder Folk Festival in Denmark. In both places, I learned that emotional truth in a song is not accessed through the facts. It's achieved by being genuine, vulnerable, and unprotected in your writing and performance.

I've sung at the grave of W.B. Yeats in Sligo, Ireland. I've played on a train that rolled nonstop for three days across Canada, from Toronto to Vancouver. I've sung in Perth, Australia, at a blues festival with a children's choir, then walked the shore by the Indian Ocean. There, thousands of miles from home, I learned that songs breathe life into a precious idea: Other people have felt and still feel the way I do.

I've learned that, at the deepest level, people in every country, in every town, in every bar, nightclub, or prison, are made of the same spiritual material. We connect at the broken places, and unite in our vulnerability. Life is precious, fragile. Songs create empathy, which unchains us, in every nation, on every continent, time and time again. ■